DRIFT

"In a *dérive*, one or more persons during a certain period drop their relations, their work and leisure activities, and all their other usual motives for movement and action, and let themselves be drawn by the attractions of the terrain and the encounters they find there."
— Guy Debord, *Theory of the Dérive*, 1958.

The translation of *dérive* is *drift*.

BERLIN

06
Masthead

07
Welcome

158
Appendix

08
Familiar Blocks
Christian Eschner

14
Coffee and Connection
Imogen Lepere

18
Kiezkultur
Dale Arden Chong

28
On The Scent
Stephanie Kramer

30
Kaffee and Kuchen
Stephanie Kramer

34
Coffee Crisis
Nina Ludolphi

44
A Roast Above
Sabrina Sucato

62
The Unlikely Coffee Kid
Eve Hill-Agnus

76
Neighborhood Vibes
Feride Yalav-Heckeroth

84
Zooming In on Neukölln
Eve Hill-Agnus

94
Coffee with Personality
Austin Langlois

106
The New Bakers of Berlin
J.R.M. Owens

122
Enjoying a Cup of עוֹאָק in Berlin
Jonathan Shipley

130
Market Days
Rachel Preece

142
Barista's Choice
Imogen Lepere

152
Operation Santa Claus
Christian Eschner

ADAM GOLDBERG
Editor in Chief

DANIELA VELASCO
Creative Director

ELYSSA GOLDBERG
Editorial Director

BONJWING LEE
Executive Editor

CONTRIBUTORS
Austin Langlois
Ben Mönks
Christian Eschner
Dale Arden Chong
Eve Hill-Agnus
Fabian Schmid
Feride Yalav-Heckeroth
Franz Grünewald
Imogen Lepere
Jack Hare
Jonathan Shipley
J.R.M. Owens
Laurel Molly
Magnus Pettersson
Maria Louceiro
Nina Ludolphi
Noel Richter
Rachel Preece
Sabrina Sucato
Stephanie Kramer

DEAR READER,

I was nine when President Reagan stood on the hem of the Iron Curtain and demanded, "Mr. Gorbachev, tear down this wall!" Mesmerized by the sea of cheering Berliners on television, I wondered about the millions who were separated from family and countrymen by the graffitied barrier that bisected the city and their hearts.

I came of age in the United States during the waning days of the Cold War. As if the final dash towards the finish line of democracy, my childhood teemed with propagandist symbols of the democratic West, which my immigrant parents, who had fled Communism, encouraged me to embrace.

Like most red-blooded, American boys of the 80s, I reveled in the freedom-fighting storylines of G.I. Joe and 007 and enthralled at the epic struggle between "us against them" pumped into the cultural zeitgeist. Cold War allegories, like the musical "Chess" (a seminal soundtrack of my youth), cemented my early allegiances to the team wearing red, white, and blue. And flag-draped movies, like "Rocky" and spy thrillers like Tom Clancy's "The Hunt for Red October" (brimming with naughty words and content deemed unfit for a child, it earned me a trip to the principal's office in third grade), drew easy, bright lines between "good guys" and "bad guys."

A world divided, being the only world I had ever known, seemed like an immutable reality at the time. Yet, astonishingly, just three years after Reagan's daring demand, I stood at the Berlin Wall chipping away at it with a pickaxe, not only dismantling a part of history, but my simple understanding of it as well. I still have those cement shards and nuggets, which, even at 12, I knew would be important mementos.

While Berlin's genealogy as the birthplace of the Prussian Empire and the Third Reich is inescapable, its denizens today seem undaunted by the long shadow of its history. I returned in 2022 to find a city that—almost in defiance of its scarred and complicated past—has blossomed into a center of cultural liberation. In the three decades since the end of Soviet occupation and my first visit, Berlin has become an unapologetic beacon of innovation, creativity, and freedom of thought, making it a favored proving ground for musicians, artists, entrepreneurs, and, of course, roasters and baristas too.

In these pages, our writers will introduce you to the various *kiezkultur*—what Dale Arden Chong describes as "neighborhood culture" in her piece about the bohemian Kreuzberg district—that help knit Berlin's yesterday with today. Christian Eschner, for example, finds coffee in revived corners of Berlin's past, from postwar tenements to an abandoned airfield that saved the city in the winter of 1948. And Eve Hill-Agnus tells us about cafes that are striving towards sustainability in Neukölln.

This thirteenth volume of Drift Magazine, like the city it explores, is dotted with monuments of acknowledgement and atonement. These thoughtful markers—like the ones in Jonathan Shipley's article about the city's Jewish heritage—deserve reflection. But the days of us against them are over. As you read, I urge you to celebrate Berlin's open arms, which have attracted an unbelievably diverse cast of people and ideas, creeds and countercultures, that, together, have pulled the city out of the penumbra of its past and into a colorful and bright, new day.

BONJWING LEE,
EXECUTIVE EDITOR

Barry McGeehin, Father Carpenter

Familiar Blocks

WORDS & PHOTOGRAPHS
Christian Eschner

Kennedy's "I am a Berliner" speech made Berlin a famous stronghold of liberty in the Western world. For a very long period of its history, however, Berlin wasn't on anyone's radar.

German cities and capitals either grew up around the seat of an archbishop, usually dominated by a large cathedral like the one in Cologne; the royal residence of a king with a royal palace, like in Munich; or they were an independent imperial city like Nuremberg, with an imperial castle and huge city walls. There was not one capital city, but many smaller ones with Cologne, Aachen, Augsburg, Regensburg, and Frankfurt having the largest populations. During most of the Holy Roman Empire, the city of Berlin wasn't worth mentioning, never having more than 12,000 inhabitants. And during the Thirty Years War in the 17th century, it lost half of its population.

However, when Berlin became the official residence of the Prussian king around 1700, the city recovered rather quickly, in part because French, Calvinist Huguenots were allowed to settle. New suburbs, like Friedrichswerder, Dorotheenstadt, and Friedrichstadt, were quickly erected to accommodate the new inhabitants. Many of them were bankers, industrialists, and investors who enjoyed luxury products and were in touch with merchants all over the world. Coffee consumption increased so quickly that it unsettled the Prussian ruler, who suspected that the coffee affected his soldiers negatively. In 1781, Frederick the Great of Prussia declared coffee a royal monopoly by royal decree to reduce an increasing amount of private coffee roasters. Much to the annoyance of the general population, he employed disabled soldiers, the so-called coffee sniffers, to spy on citizens who were illegally roasting coffee to avoid the high taxes assessed on coffee and other luxury items.

About 100 years after Frederick the Great's coffee decree, the German states were united under Emperor Wilhelm I, who made his home in Berlin, by then, firmly established as the capital of Prussia. In the meantime, Berlin had become an industrial city with 800,000 inhabitants, with a modern subway system and new tenement blocks accommodating the new working masses.

Because of this sudden increase of industrial power and late urban development, Berlin's residential districts developed differently than other capital cities, like London, which consisted of low-rise houses. In Berlin, residential housing tended to be taller, heftier, and square-shaped tenements divided into the tiniest apartments for families of six to 10. Often concealed behind elaborate façades decorated by elements from Late Classical to Neo-Baroque periods, these complexes of courtyards stretched far back within the blocks of brick. Because of poor sanitation and Prussia's focus on military endeavors, the blocks bear the distinctive name of *mietskasernen*, or rental barracks, and have come to define much of Berlin's appearance today. The courtyards served as squares, where families met and politics were discussed. Often coffee roasters took advantage of the warren of enclosed spaces to supply the working class with clandestine caffeine. Intellectual minds like the Grimm Brothers, Karl Marx, and Heinrich Heine met in these hidden cafes. Conveniently, the maze of courtyards also helped make Berlin a burgeoning headquarter for national labor organizations and offered safer spaces for meetings of all stripes, including mixed-religion crowds.

In the decades after World War II, the tenement blocks proliferated in the East, creating an environment that was closely aligned with the German Democratic Republic's (or GDR, the

official name of Soviet-controlled East Germany) socio-political goals. The so-called slab blocks in East Berlin, then the capital of the GDR, on the one hand, are remembered for the bleakness, shoddy workmanship, and forced collectivism of that socialist era. On the other hand, they also represent the ideals of the GDR: social equity, low rents, and a narrower gap between rich and poor, which helped make those courtyards a meeting space for East Berliners. Especially in non-conformist districts like Prenzlauer Berg and Friedrichshain or in the dilapidated parts of Mitte, people met there for readings, drank coffee together, and even attended backyard punk concerts.

Because of a lack of supply due to Soviet restrictions, coffee became a scarce commodity in the eastern zones. But demand remained high, and only increased after the GDR forced a coffee mix, which was made up of only 51% coffee, diluted by pea flour, chicory, and several beans, on East German citizens in the late 1970s. So, coffee sent from friends and family members in West Germany constituted about 20% of the GDR's coffee. Whereas GDR's party-privileged residents living in the apartment buildings of the grand boulevard Karl-Marx-Allee (dubbed the "Champs Elysée of the East") could afford to visit places like Café Sibylle, common workers couldn't. If they didn't have any relatives in West Germany, who could send them coffee; or knew anyone with the right to travel to the West, who could bring back coffee for them; or they were unwilling to exchange their own currency for *Deutsche Marks* at a horrendous black market rate in order to buy Western coffee, a rare taste of freedom might be found in the courtyards of East Berliners' tenement blocks, where they could enjoy someone's freshly brewed coffee.

After reunification of East and West Germany, the tenement blocks—long reviled, but now intensely sought—house fewer and fewer working class families today. The spirit of the courtyards however hasn't changed. Father Carpenter opened in 2015 in one of the many courtyards of Mitte, in former East Berlin. The building once housed a cigar factory and craft shops like a butchery, so Kresten Thøgersen—owner of Father Carpenter and Fjord Coffee Roasters—named this brunch cafe as an homage to his father's profession. The blue tiles on the walls are original to the former store—the building being a historically protected monument, changes to the structure are now almost impossible. Thøgersen however appreciates the craftsmanship background and the vicinity of the neighborhood. Migrating from Melbourne to realize his idea of a cafe, he has quickly found his place in Berlin's coffee community, which, especially in Mitte, is flourishing. "One of the owners of Five Elephant, Kris [Schackman], is a good friend of mine. Both he and I are not from Germany, so whenever there is a problem with [the] German regulatory office or the German taxation system, he and I are trying to figure out the problem together."

Only a few steps away, Wissem Ben Rahim opened his cafe Ben Rahim in the very same year as Thøgersen opened his cafe in the nearby courtyard Hackesche Höfe. In emphasizing his own Arab heritage and hospitality he has managed to transform a former soap factory into a third wave coffee shop with an Arab twist. By serving Arab beverages like *ibrik*, he wants his customers to feel a combination of Tunisian hospitality and the familiarity of the courtyards of Berlin. Ben Rahim offers Berliners a peaceful escape within the labyrinth of tenement courtyards before they head out into the stressful reality of modern Berlin.

Today's baristas don't feel any competition among their third wave coffee houses in Berlin. "Rising tide lifts all boats," Thøgersen says. "There are enough customers for all of us."

Within the protective walls of a courtyard, Thøgersen has tried to gather neighbors and office workers alike. Families from the apartments above enjoy breakfast or lunch there, and his 90-second rule between ordering and delivering coffee allows workers to be back at their desks after a short coffee break.

"In Berlin, it's easier to ask for forgiveness than to ask for permission," Thøgersen has learned. Before opening his own roastery, he was test roasting in the hidden courtyard of Father Carpenter. Neighbors wondered what the unknown smell was, so they came around sniffing, he remembers. This might have spelled disaster 240 years ago during the reign of Frederick the Great. But today, especially after having endured the oppression of the GDR's totalitarian political system during the Cold War, Berliners are focusing on coming together, and Berlin's tenement blocks provide the perfect place to confide in and support one another.

—

Coffee and Connection

WORDS
Imogen Lepere

PHOTOGRAPHS
Fabian Schmid

Few things have the power to brighten our day as quickly as walking into a beloved cafe, greeting the barista and seeing them make our favorite coffee before we've even ordered it. Anyone who has spent time in a new city knows that having a regular coffee spot and a rapport with the people who work there is one of the quickest ways to feel rooted—no matter how different that city is from our own. However, imagine how much more vital this familiarity is for refugees who've been forced to flee their homes and find themselves in an alien place with no connections and limited financial resources.

This is the thinking behind Refugio Café, a relaxed spot on Lenaustrasse in the Neukölln neighborhood. It's owned by Berlin City Mission and run entirely by volunteers. The cafe looks like the many other achingly hip joints in Neukölln: a glass case of house-baked cakes is perched on a counter made from upcycled packing cases, vases display beautiful dried flower arrangements, and an arty crowd sips flat whites while hovering over laptops.

Refugio was born in response to the refugee crisis of 2015, which saw over a million Syrians flee to Germany to avoid war. Although it was intended as a place where they could learn hospitality and language skills, it has become so much more. Nowadays, it's an eclectic ecosystem, where refugees and asylum seekers, international students and the liberal locals who call Neukölln home meet and mingle. What they share is an understanding of the value of community—and a love for specialty coffee.

"The cafe was always imagined as the melting pot between the outside and inside world and that's still what it is," says manager, Anna Pass. "The building itself is home to several small NGOs [non-governmental organizations], such as Bikeygees, which teaches women how to ride bicycles, as well as a [boarding] house, where up to 40 newly arrived refugees live until they're able to support themselves."

Eyad Agha fled Syria after surviving several life-threatening events and now lives at Refugio House and uses the cafe like a living room. Although he has a full time job elsewhere, he credits his time volunteering at Refugio with introducing him to coffee culture and it still plays an important role in his social life.

"I can't imagine living in Berlin without the cafe," says Agha. "I spend so many hours working here on my laptop and catching up with friends as well as making new ones. You always meet people from very different backgrounds with interesting stories and experiences."

Home to the KINDL Centre for Contemporary Art, as well as a host of independent galleries and vintage shops, such as Sing Blackbird, Neukölln is one of the most diverse districts in Berlin. More than 20% of the city's Arab residents call it home and their presence can be felt in Turkish bakeries such as Taktil and the street food stalls on Maybach Ufer, which sell pomegranate juice and piquant falafel wraps as thick as one's forearm. However, according to Emma Ramsey, a history student from New Zealand and Refugio volunteer, few offer an atmosphere as welcoming as Refugio.

"The whole premise of the cafe is that it is a community space that belongs to everyone," Ramsey muses. "It's a front entrance to so many other community projects happening within the building—it's a real hive of activity. People can come in to take a breath, they can order food, or simply pop in for a friendly conversation as they pass by. I think social spaces like these are so important, particularly in big cities where it is very easy to feel overwhelmed and alone."

Every year, Refugio hosts a community party for its birthday as well as regular live music events and a Christmas market, where residents sell homemade crafts and food. But it's the cafe that provides the daily moments of connection that are so precious to its regulars.

"Coffee is communication," says Pass. "It provides a moment to pause, reflect, and connect with ourselves and those around us. We're located on a small side street, so anyone who comes here has sought us out because they share our values. We meet everyone as equals here. Yes, volunteers learn practical skills but it's the human interaction that really changes their lives."

—

Rafael Rosa, Refugio Café

Geumah Lee, Refugio Café

Annelies

Kiezkultur

WORDS
Dale Arden Chong

PHOTOGRAPHS
Noel Richter

Every city has its slice of bohemia, but none seems to have one quite as notable as Berlin. As Germany's largest city, both in size and population, there is no shortage of artists, musicians, writers, and other members of the creative class here. As a result, the country's capital has become a place where many push away from commercial businesses—including localized franchises—and flock to their small, independent community shops instead.

"Most people who came to Berlin came here to reinvent themselves and find the individual way that suits them. It's a lot about being creative and not following the mainstream opinions," Jutta Tischendorf, the founder of her eponymous coffee shop Tischendorf—located on Friedelstrasse in Reuterkiez—shared. "The same thing applies to their way of spending money. [Berliners] would rather support a small company that supports local artists and is a part of the community rather than a big fish."

According to Tischendorf, who opened her business in 2012, a lot has changed in Berlin's coffee scene over the past decade. "We have more chains and bigger businesses than a few years ago…it used to be a bit more free and easy when I started," she explained. A businesswoman, who sought to enrich the city's coffee culture after spending nearly four years enjoying coffee in Sydney, Australia, she notes that Berlin's level of hospitality has also become more international due to the high number of expats moving to the city, attracted by the growing economy.

It comes as no surprise, then, larger companies would consider putting roots down. In 2018, Google planned to build a new campus in the neighborhood of Kreuzberg, which was historically home to "punks and anarchists," according to Tischendorf. Local residents fought against the presence of the tech company, ultimately winning the battle. Although this didn't prevent Google from building a campus in the city, it did demonstrate the neighborhood's values and preference for small companies, like independent coffee shops. "Nobody can stop the gentrification, but at least you can decide who you want to support." Hannes Haake, the co-owner of Distrikt Coffee on Bergstrasse and Annelies on Görlitzer, believes that locals have always supported independent businesses. "There's a charm to a lot of unique bars, cafes, and shops where you have the feeling that owners express themselves more for fun than in a business sense," he said. As a result, they tend to avoid the idea of money-focused franchises, noting the opening of a Starbucks near Distrikt that closed months later due to a lack of business. "It shows that Berlin has a strong identity and it makes me confident that the city will be able to keep its self acclaimed vibe called 'poor but sexy.'"

One coffee shop owner saw this dispute with big tech up close and personal. "Given the left-leaning nature of Berlin, it makes sense that the locals kind of band together and force the things they don't want out," said Amanda Ceccato, the co-owner of Kaffeebar in Graefekiez, which is located just around the corner from Kreuzberg.

Kiezkultur—neighborhood culture—is really strong in this city. Ceccato suggested that this is because residents support everything in the areas where they live, and they have everything close to their homes. Maintaining this, though, takes a conscious effort from everyone. "I think everyone working together to support the places they want to succeed, even if it's inconvenient at the time, really makes the difference," she shared. "We all know this place isn't like a 'normal city,' and if you're committed to making this place home, you quickly identify that this is how

you have to be to keep things going in the right direction—it's your responsibility."

Kiezkultur may be something that starts with a neighborhood's locals, but it extends to relationships between businesses, as well. "During difficult times and crises, we all had to learn the hard way that you can't make it on your own. Community feels much better than making sure you are only saving your boat," Tischendorf, who adds that she and her business were in an exchange with a large group of cafe owners to discuss how to handle the impact of the pandemic, said. "Everyone in high-quality food and hospitality is fighting an uphill battle," Gabe Dunn, a Berlin resident who works in sales at the Norwegian green coffee importer Nordic Approach, stated. "If your business is among those that last, you're basically in an exclusive club of war vets."

Berlin's close-knit network of small business owners, whether they be coffee shops or businesses focusing on other goods or services, makes it easy for them to support each other. "From the start we felt like one could always reach out to other local businesses to ask for guidance which was always a nice feeling. It's still like that and our door is always open when people reach out for help or guidance," Haake shared. This often manifests in the form of cafes stocking bottles from the local wine shop or pastries from the neighborhood bakery. Ceccato also shared that working through the last two years reinforced the overall support from the community as a whole and now encourages her to pay it forward. "When I visit my favorite cafes, I also buy my wine or some cookies for later, because I know from the other side what a difference these sales make."

The investment in community and relationships comes full circle when Berlin's coffee shop owners also support their customers. Occasionally, this is done by showcasing the works of the artists, musicians, and writers who stop by to work or simply enjoy the coffee and food. Other times, it's by involving them in the businesses. "Earnestness and transparency are key. The current economic and utility crises have forced most small cafes to raise their prices significantly, and many of the cafes responded by taking to social media to share a precise breakdown of why, including the cost of goods, labor, and more," Dunn explained when discussing how Berlin's coffee shops connect with their visitors. "To me, this communicates a degree of respect… treating [customers] like… collaborators rather than [just] customers."

This mutual respect and support between Berlin's independently owned coffee shops and their customers—as well as that between the owners and their teams—might be the best example of Berliners leveraging their shared value to lift up small businesses and unconventional thinkers, moving everyone forward. And it's this collective sense of community and responsibility for independence that makes the city's coffee culture quintessentially Berlin.

—

On The Scent

WORDS
Stephanie Kramer

ILLUSTRATION
Laurel Molly

Nowadays, holding a cup of coffee and savoring its amazing scent doesn't seem like a dangerous thing to do. But back in 18th century Prussia, this simple pleasure could have cost you. Although the first coffee house opened in Bremen in 1673, coffee struggled for years against prohibitions and bans. Berlin, the capital of Prussia since 1701, was the last major German city to open a coffee shop.

The main reason was opposition from Frederick the Great, then king of Prussia. In 1721 the king allowed a cafe to open at the palace in the *lustgarten*, or "pleasure garden." Coffee was reserved for a small circle of state officials, royalty, and the elite—and the king intended to keep it that way.

The Prussian economy was floundering, and coffee was an expensive import. But, while it was initially drunk by the upper classes, its popularity grew and more people began switching from beer to coffee—a trend that was particularly distressing for local beer brewers. The king claimed that he had been raised on a diet of *biersuppe* (beer soup) and advised his subjects to keep consuming it morning, noon, and night. In 1781 he imposed a luxury tax on coffee and monopolized the coffee trade, granting permits only to a handful of state-run roasteries.

But the ruler failed to anticipate the inventiveness and resourcefulness of his people. They didn't stop drinking coffee—they only stopped doing so legally. To evade the tax, smugglers hid coffee beans between bales of hay and stacks of wood. The trading of green coffee beans also increased, as they were taxed at a lower rate and didn't have an easily distinguishable smell—and people could roast them secretly on their stove tops at home.

Coffee continued to be a thorn in the king's side, but he did not give up. To enforce the ban on illegal roasting, he employed 400 "coffee sniffers," war veterans who went door-to-door searching for illegal roasters and fining those they caught. The coffee police were authorized to enter people's homes and could even stop men and women on the street and conduct bodily searches. As employees of the king, they were highly paid and received a hefty bonus when they were successful. Given coffee's distinctive aroma, they were indeed very successful, if not also unpopular.

The coffee sniffers were finally disbanded in 1787 after the king died and his successor took over. The new ruler realized he was no match for coffee, and that trying to contain the black market was costing the state far more than it gained through taxing open trade.

Today, about 80% of Germans over age 14 say they drink coffee. Coffee culture is thriving, with third wave cafes popping up on every corner of Berlin. Some of them, such as Röststätte and 19grams, even offer training courses (in German and English) to help you brew the perfect cup at home. And these days there's no need to fear that a knock at the door might be a uniformed official—you're free to enjoy every drop of it!

Ben Rahim

Kaffee and Kuchen

WORDS
Stephanie Kramer

PHOTOGRAPHS
Noel Richter

Berliners are known for their love of beer, sausage, and sauerkraut. But spend some time exploring the historic capital of Germany and you'll discover another tradition: coffee and cake. In this once-divided city, *kaffee* and *kuchen* have remained together for over 200 years. Cafes provide a place for slowing down, getting together with friends or family, and having a leisurely chat while indulging in an afternoon treat. This ritual is so important to German identity that there's even a word for it: *kaffeeklatsch* ("coffee chat").

The word *klatsch* means "clap," "chatter," or "gossip." After the first coffee houses opened in Berlin during the 17th century, salons flourished as places where the intellectual elite met to exchange ideas or debate political and cultural views. As coffee became more affordable in the 1800s, more people gathered at home or in cafes for coffee, cake, and conversation. Newspapers from the 1890s reported on the emergence of the *kaffeeklatsch*, a new trend that would eventually become a tradition.

Today, the centuries-old custom remains near and dear to German hearts. Strict trading laws in Berlin require stores to close on Sundays, but coffee shops and bakeries can stay open.

***
Anna Blume

Located on a leafy side street in upscale Prenzlauer Berg, Anna Blume is a cafe, bakery, and flower shop all in one. Named after a poem by Kurt Schwitters, its walls are decorated with whimsical drawings and verses from his 1919 Dadaist work. Burgundy leather banquettes, heavy red drapes, and abundant floral arrangements create a unique atmosphere that is both elegant and cozy.

The large outdoor patio provides a space where you can people-watch or observe the florists through a window while they work. When the weather turns colder, the candlelit warmth and the sweet scent of flowers invite you inside to spend a relaxing hour or two. Near the entrance is a long glass vitrine filled with authentic German sweets like crumb cake, marble cake, and sour cherry tart. Choose from up to 18 different varieties to go alongside your Black Forest coffee, rose petal tea, or Belgian hot chocolate.

***
Ben Rahim

When Tunisian-born Ben Rahim opened his eponymous cafe in Berlin in 2015, he dreamed of blending third wave specialty coffee with his own cultural heritage. He found the perfect spot in the historical Hackesche Höfe, a complex of beautifully renovated courtyard buildings in the heart of Berlin's touristy Mitte district.

Tucked away in a quiet corner, this hidden gem has just enough space for a short row of checkerboard-sized wooden tables along one wall. The stylish interior is decorated with Tunisian lamps, mosaics, and a large, ornately carved wooden mirror at the end of the bar. A shaded terrace with a colorfully tiled fountain provides a lovely oasis for taking a break from the shopping crowds.

The cafe's signature drink is brewed in an *ibrik*, one of the oldest brewing methods in the world. Milk and sugar are discouraged—unless you order a latte or flat white—so that you can taste the flavor notes.

Coffee, or *mocca*, is traditionally served with a date. It's also exquisitely paired with one of the excellent Middle Eastern delicacies such as *namoura*, a tangy semolina square sweetened with honey.

***
Café Einstein

A Berlin institution, Café Einstein is one of the city's grandest coffee houses. Step inside this 19th century villa, with its high ceilings, marble-topped tables, and newspapers hanging on wooden holders, and you're immediately transported back in time. Dressed in traditional black and white, the waitstaff is known to discourage cell phone use. But as you soak up the special atmosphere of this prewar relic, you can almost imagine the centuries of conversations over coffee and cake.

Café Einstein roasts its famous Viennese blend in Berlin, boasting 20 varieties of coffee from four continents. The results are highly complex blends with aromas ranging from earthy and spicy to sweet and fruity. Luxurious cakes and desserts include chunky apple strudel, *Sachertorte*, and other tempting selections.

The coffee scene in Berlin is exploding. But as newcomers pop up alongside established cafes, both are offering a contemporary take on a timeless tradition. If you want to get away from the hustle and bustle of modern city life, a *kaffeeklatsch* was and is a wonderful way to idle away an afternoon.

Café Sybille

Coffee Crisis

WORDS
Nina Ludolphi

PHOTOGRAPHS
Noel Richter

In 1976 a bad coffee harvest in Brazil sent shockwaves through international markets. In East Berlin, then capital of the German Democratic Republic (GDR), this set in motion curious events in the highest echelons of the socialist government. The country's economy was centrally planned and largely state-owned, which meant that everything from development and production to pricing and marketing of goods was managed by GDR agencies. And so in 1977 it fell upon state officials to find solutions for a looming shortage of coffee beans as the state's currency reserves were squeezed by skyrocketing coffee bean prices.

The stakes were surprisingly high for such a seemingly mundane commodity. If consumers in the state-owned shops, institutions and offices, canteens, restaurants, and cafes across the land would have to go without coffee, their frustration would eventually be directed at the central government. After all, coffee was held in high regard among GDR consumers, an everyday staple, a symbol of stability and humble luxury. Ever concerned with the leadership's public standing, the GDR's top politicians, among them chairman of the State Council and head of state Erich Honecker, got to work.

Already more than 20% of the country's annual coffee needs (more than 10 tons annually) were covered by gifts and private parcels from the West. Import duty restrictions were loosened to keep this incoming flow of beans steady. Behind the scenes, trade and barter deals with friendly coffee producing nations were intensified, a key factor in Vietnam becoming a major producer for Robusta beans today. But none of these measures could solve the supply issues the GDR was facing without simultaneous efforts to manage the demand.

Coffee brands in West Germany navigated the rising prices for green beans by introducing products containing coffee beans and surrogate ingredients to meet a steady consumer demand for affordable coffee products. An eerie reminder of post-war scarcity and coffee surrogates, maybe this strategy was the solution?

Just across from Berlin's iconic radio tower, the former House of Statistics is now a graffiti-covered relic of Berlin's past. Back then the building on the corner of the prestigious Karl-Marx-Allee housed the offices of different GDR government agencies. There, high up on the eighth floor in room 820, Werner Wienert, now in his eighties, became involved in what was later dubbed the *Kaffeekrise* (coffee crisis) of the late 1970s. In his role as the director of the hospitality sector in the Ministry for Trade and Supply he found himself in the middle of the nation's leaders' efforts to navigate the crisis. His task: to develop and distribute a new coffee surrogate to stretch supplies. The order came from the party's central committee complete with a name for the new product: *Kaffee-Mix*. Food engineers at the state-operated Institute for Grain Processing near Berlin whipped up a recipe of reportedly 51% coffee beans and 49% surrogates (roasted grains, pea proteins, chicory root, among other ingredients), "probably within a few days," Wienert recalls, and the product underwent internal testing. The mixture infamously wreaked havoc on some of the commercial coffee makers when it clogged filters and caused the large machines to malfunction and even explode. According to Wienert, they later launched a tweaked version of the recipe to avoid these issues.

A cupping for taste among ministry officials included several other coffee products, including the competitor coffee surrogate *Jota-Sport* from the West. "The results? Completely unusable,

Café Sybille

they were all over the place," remembers Wienert. Yet, despite the lack of consensus, the state officials unanimously decided to move forward with their product in summer of 1977. In a state-wide effort, popular low-price coffee products were taken off the shelves and replaced with the new state-approved *Kaffee-Mix*. Faced with the decision between expensive higher quality products or the budget-friendly surrogate, consumers often opted for the latter, many of them disgruntled and feeling that this switch was forced upon them by the state without warning or explanation. This negative sentiment was intensified by the fact that most state-owned canteens and hospitality ventures now only offered the *Kaffee-Mix*, so that many in the working class had to buy the surrogate brew or go without coffee at all. Selected upscale shops, cafes, and hotels still offered regular coffee, which was an additional cause for public criticism. Numerous consumer complaints concerning the *Kaffee-Mix* were filed with state-operated businesses and state agencies all over the GDR. From "no coffee aroma" to "disgrace" and "mess," they didn't mince words.

Meanwhile in Berlin, the infamous Ministry for State Security (the GDR's secret police) monitored the growing discontent closely and reported its concerns to the party leadership. By then, the public discussion about coffee was threatening to amalgamate with criticism of the GDR as a whole. When pressure became too much the product was quietly discontinued in January of 1978. Looking back on these events, Werner Wienert still regrets the decision to radically replace two popular coffee products in the affordable price segment with *Kaffee-Mix* and describes the outcome of this gung-ho product launch as "tragic." According to him, it was not the allegedly subpar taste of *Kaffee-Mix* that riled up people against their government but the fact that they were deprived of the opportunity to choose. His brief analysis of the product's failure shows why the coffee crisis to this day is seen as an analogy to the GDR's complex political and economical dynamics.

Now, more than 45 years later, few traces of the GDR coffee crisis can be found in Berlin beyond archives, anecdotes, and rare flea market finds, such as old *Kaffee-Mix* packages. However, some cafes and bars of East Berlin's prestigious boulevard Karl-Marx-Allee can still be visited today. Salon Babette, sister location to the impressive former Café Moskau (now an event space) serves cocktails and coffee specialties (among them, a coffee surrogate) in a mid-century glass cube space. Across the street, Berlinale film festival location Kino International offers sweeping views of the boulevard at its wood-paneled Panorama Bar complete with 1960s chandeliers and matching armchairs. And a little further down the road, the once swanky Café Sybille is now a cozy landmark with historic murals and exhibitions about the country's socialist past.

—

A Roast Above

WORDS
Sabrina Sucato

PHOTOGRAPHS
Magnus Pettersson

Is it any wonder that Berlin's roasting scene draws close parallels to Germany's luxury car industry? In a country known for covetable carmakers like Audi, BMW, Mercedes-Benz, and Porsche, the fact that its capital city showcases an exceptional commitment to top-quality roasting makes perfect sense. After all, there are more than a few similarities between the two industries: precision, attention to detail, and a focus on quality.

Take THE BARN, for instance. One of the biggest names in Berlin's roasting scene, THE BARN is also one of the oldest. The company, which was founded by Ralf Rueller in 2010, came onto the scene before the city boasted the interest in specialty coffee that it does today.

"There was no reference for quality in Germany at the time when I opened THE BARN," Rueller notes. "It was a clear gap on the coffee map, and I filled it."

True to his word, Rueller makes this commitment to quality apparent in all THE BARN does. The company focuses on single-origin coffees sourced from farms with which it has personal relationships. In 2012, Rueller started working directly with farm partners and now visits each farmer once a year to help them level up their quality. All coffee at THE BARN must score 86 points or higher on the Specialty Coffee Association's 100-point scale and is served black, without sugar, to help customers "slow down and experience the clean flavors of the fields so they can connect to the farm through their taste," Rueller explains. "What we hear very often from our customers is that in the evening they can still remember our coffee that they had in the morning."

For Rueller, the secret to success at THE BARN is focusing on less and making products better and better with each turn. With 10 individually designed specialty coffee shops in Berlin, not to mention a handful across the globe and a thriving online business that ships to 82 countries, he's clearly onto something.

"We want our customers to slow down and explore the full potential of specialty coffee," he says. "THE BARN is a different coffee experience."

Another roastery working to elevate coffee culture in Berlin is Röststätte. The family business came to life in 2010 when Yvonne and Ivo Weller founded it after previously running a premium espresso machine company since 2003. In the years that followed, Röststätte developed a reputation for balanced, precise roasts and, more recently, innovative coffee products. Using its Loring S35 Kestrel roaster, the company crafts something to suit every sort of espresso and filter coffee craving. Röststätte also makes what Dominic Ottlinger, Yvonne's son and head of marketing for the company, calls "a damn good cold brew coffee liqueur" sold as Cold Brew X.

"We are always innovating with our coffee," Ottlinger enthuses. "In general, we give our colleagues the opportunities to develop and implement ideas."

That potential for ideation has proven successful for Röststätte, which has taken home wins at the German Barista Championship, the German Brewers Cup, and the Good Spirits Championship, and made it to the finalist stage of multiple World Coffee Championships. As for distributing its beans, in addition to serving them at its roastery and cafe locations, Röststätte also maintains a thriving website operation and partners with businesses and restaurants throughout the region. Recently, Ottlinger notes that the brand has seen a growing interest in the office sector as well.

THE BARN

Jin Won Yang & Luke Yang, THE BARN

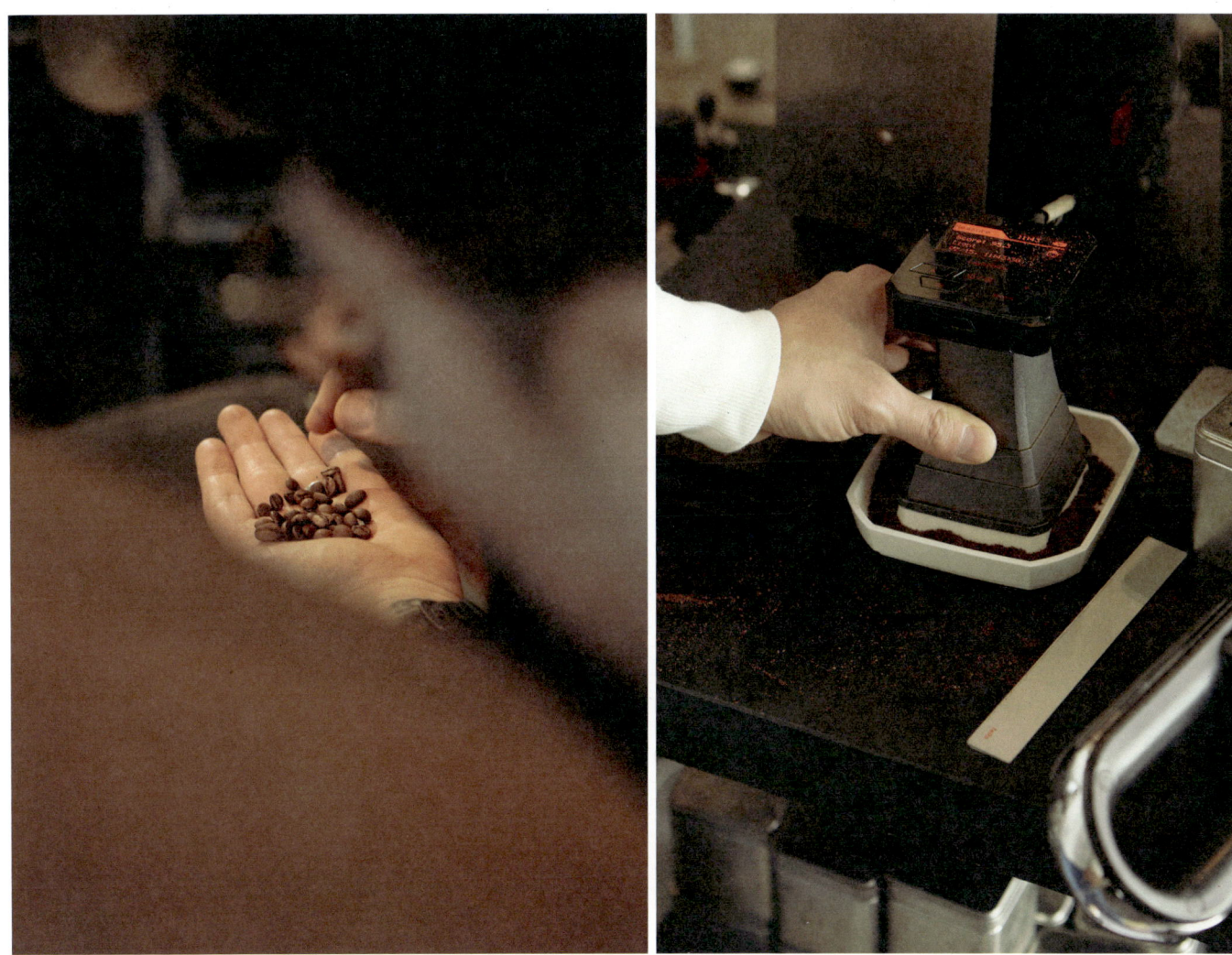

Garreth Druce, THE BARN

Junko Chida, THE BARN

THE BARN

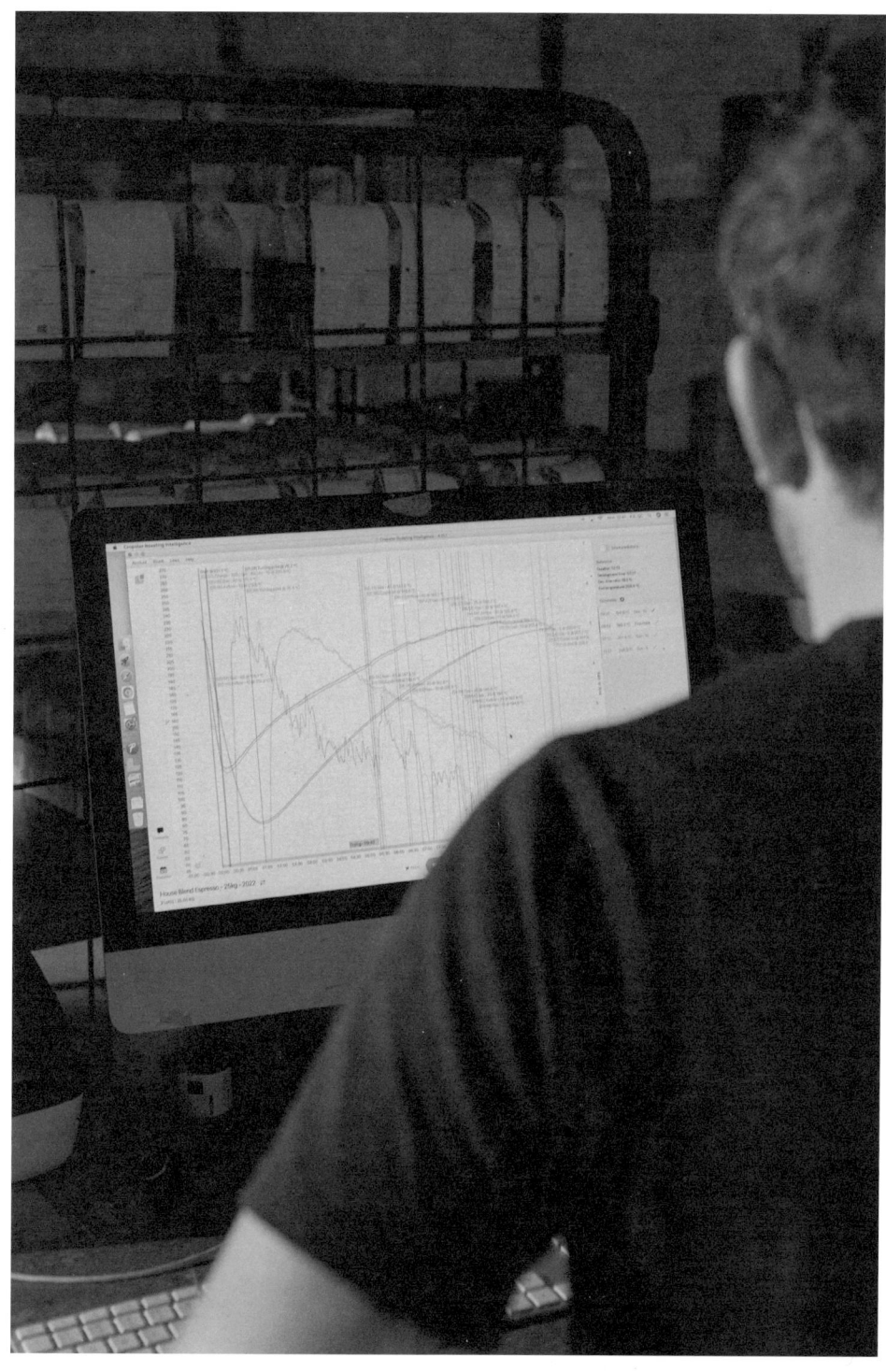

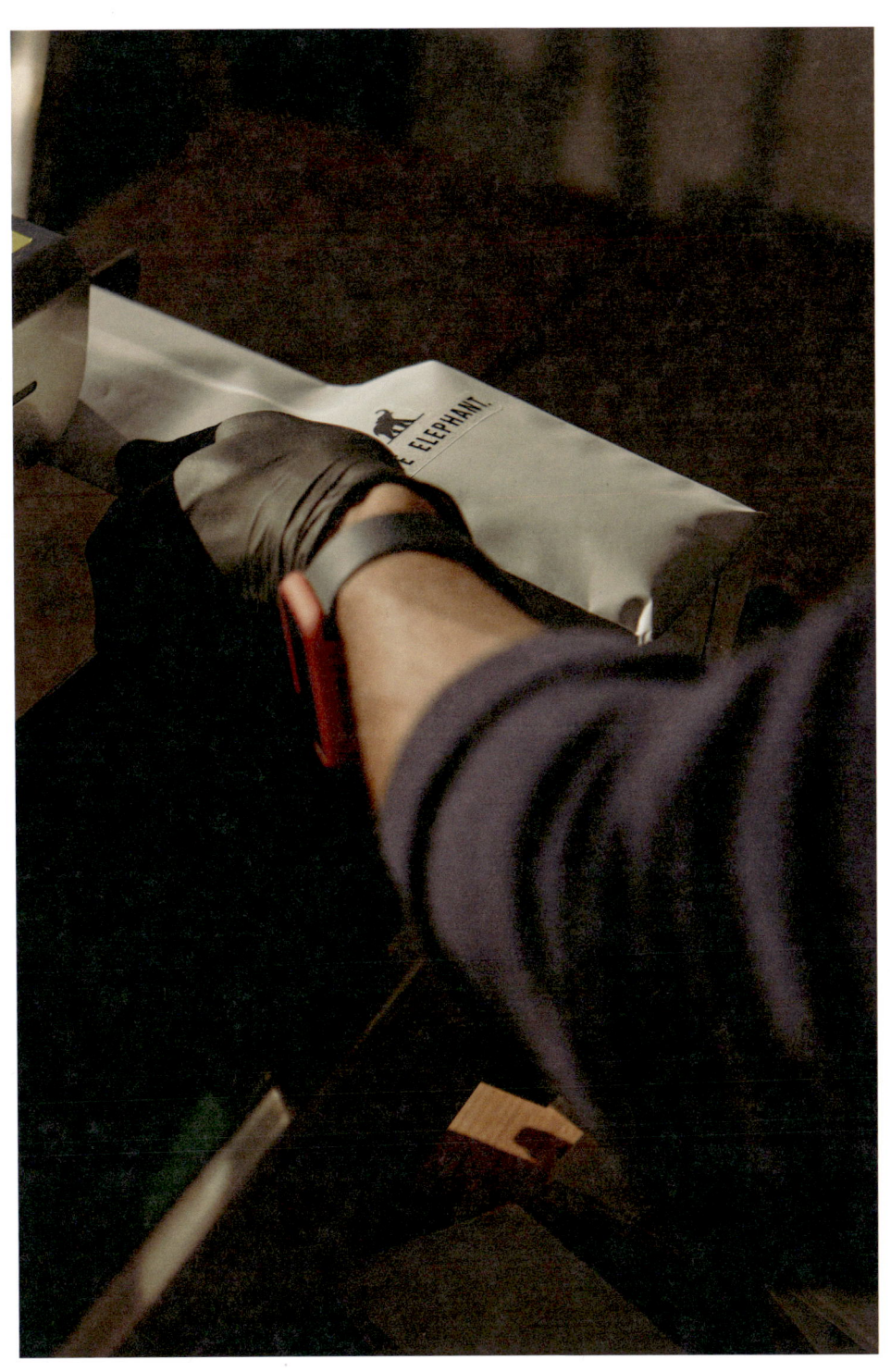

Thomas Maskovich, Five Elephant

"We love the spirit and the diversity of our hometown and the opportunity to grow and develop our idea of hospitality together with guests and customers," Ottlinger says.

Like Röststätte, Five Elephant also got its start in Berlin in 2010. With a focus on specialty coffee that emphasizes taste just as much as it does environmental impact, the brand has carved a niche for itself in the city. At its multiple locations, coffee aficionados can sip on varieties that support sustainable partnerships with growers as far afield as Colombia, El Salvador, Ethiopia, and Kenya. Due to popular demand, Five Elephant has expanded to offer global shipping of its beans, along with monthly subscriptions that feature a rotating selection of single-origin roasts. With each roast release, Five Elephant tells the stories of the farmers behind the beans. It educates just as much as it inspires, feeding the community with knowledge, warmth, and, of course, excellent cups of java.

That emphasis on customer, and, on a larger scale, community service is also apparent at Fjord Coffee Roasters. Notably, Fjord is the result of a unique partnership between Father Carpenter and Silo, which, prior to Fjord's founding in 2016, were in the process of opening their own roasteries. Instead of competing with one another, they chose to join forces to create a single top-quality roastery. Today, that roastery distributes to cafes across Berlin, including Distrikt and Silo Coffee, among others.

"The central idea of founding Fjord was to have a roasting company that ticked more than one box," explains Jordan Montgomery, the roastery manager. For founders Kresten Thøgersen, Morgan Love, and James Maguire, those boxes included the highest level of quality that was measurable, holistic partnerships, support, and positive outcomes. Over the years, Fjord has done just that, developing both business-to-business and direct-to-consumer programs in Berlin and across the globe.

Fjord focuses on rare, exotic, and unique coffees that are often difficult to find.

"Rather than purchase, roast, and sell coffees that are easy or cheaper to obtain, we seek out what we think is the best expression of a particular origin, region, varietal, and so on," Montgomery notes. "We believe that the cleaner the profile of the coffee, the better the consumer is able to experience and appreciate the unique qualities it has."

When it comes to roasting, Fjord employs different roasters for sampling (the 50g Ikawa), production (the 12kg Probat), and rare and exotic coffees (1kg Bullet). This process allows the team to determine the best course of action for each roast and ensure that each customer receives roasts that are as fresh as possible.

"We approach roasting as a delicate and high-level science, and we spend much of our time each week undertaking rigorous quality control, test roasts, and calibration sessions to ensure that we are experts in our craft," Montgomery says. If it sounds like a lot, that's because it is. Yet this commitment to detail and quality are part of Fjord's DNA, and the company wouldn't have it any other way. Based upon its success with distribution throughout Germany and across the globe, its customers wouldn't either.

"Although a majority of coffee consumption is still at a commodity level, specialty coffee in Germany has grown phenomenally in the last 10 years," Montgomery enthuses. "We're proud to not only be part of this amazing growth, but to help educate and convert coffee drinkers to higher quality coffee."

Bonanza Coffee Roasters—Mitte

The Unlikely Coffee Kid

WORDS
Eve Hill-Agnus

PHOTOGRAPHS
Magnus Pettersson

Kiduk Reus came to coffee the long way. He can tell you about the vast field of publishing and advertising design in which he worked, and about Gouda, the cheese of his family's hometown. Just as easily, he'll recount the tale behind the vintage Probat model roaster that graces one of the most attractive coffee roasteries in Berlin. That's because it's a proxy for his own story as the city's unlikely third wave coffee kid, who founded Berlin's original, avant-garde roastery. Today, Bonanza Coffee's reach is wide, supplying Michelin-starred restaurants Kin Dee and CODA in Berlin, for example, as well as a coffee roasting facility and multiple cafe locations in Seoul..

When Reus opened the Oderbergerstrasse location of Bonanza Coffee in 2006, he was among the first third wave specialty coffee trailblazers in Europe. Korean-born and adopted by an American mother and Dutch father, he grew up in the Netherlands and studied design at Willem de Kooning Academy in Rotterdam and then Rietveld Academy of Arts in Amsterdam. By the 1990s, he was working in a Dutch capital that was booming with advertising, but he was disenchanted and had been, as he says, "fiddling around" with coffee.

He arrived in Berlin ahead of the coming of the third wave of coffee, which had just begun spreading across the globe—Berlin would be slow in awakening to it.

The force and engine that launched his roastery's thousand ships was an early UG series, cast-iron Probat roaster. It beckoned from a shed near the Probat factory, discovered by a happy accident, and was sold to Reus by a descendant of the Probat family.

Reus, who would influence early roasters as the third wave emerged in Berlin, had learned from obsessively researching online, home barista forums—the niche pockets of cutting-edge information at the time—that cast-iron boasted better heat transfer and durability. "When you want to roast coffee, you want to go up and down with the heat," he explains, which cast iron allows roasters to do nimbly.

As the specialty coffee culture took off, with its new insistence on subtler flavors, the whole world seemed in search of sources that could feed an appetite for the vintage equipment, refurbished, with its distinctive locomotive-shaped funnel top and gas-fueled circular drum.

Reus carved out a space for himself as the man in Berlin handling the equipment everyone wanted: organically, he became known as the Germany-based, multilingual Probat whisperer, retrofitting the German-made antiques to suit the new needs of third wave roasters. These were different from those of roasters when the machines were built in the 1920s, 30s, 50s, or 60s: a more delicate, light roast; greater roasting capacity; and far more gadgets and control.

Importantly, he looped in the *main-d'oeuvre*, a growing stable of mechanics who could handle the job on both technical and aesthetic levels.

"When I stepped in, because I was also a roaster, I knew exactly what needed to be done with that equipment." He would tell his technicians, "The burner has to have this capacity. You have to add power. Could you put a pressure gauge on the drum so we can gauge air-flow speed?" He checked for and insisted on simple things, like having the bearings properly tightened, "so the machine wouldn't be wobbling when switched on"—which

Ronan Crix, Bonanza Coffee Roasters—Mitte

Kiduk Reus, Bonanza Coffee Roasters

Thawanporn "Kai" Vorasiwa, Bonanza Coffee Roasters—Adalbertstr

Anna Chirkina, Bonanza Coffee Roasters—Oderberger

affects the machine's longevity—and that a new coat of paint would suit a more modern look.

"So many people wanted this equipment," he says. "Because I could speak all the languages"—German, English, Dutch—"that's how I could help people. I realized there was a market and need and interest for this." He became a polyglot middleman.

The Bonanza handprint was felt from Australia to Brooklyn.

In the Bonanza shop and production headquarters on Adalbertstrasse in Kreutzberg that Reus opened 10 years after his first cafe, the original, three-kilo vintage roaster is still in rotation in a space designed by the Berlin-based firm Modiste.

"How can we make it so that it's a bit unusual?" Reus wondered about the space, which functions as a roastery and flagship cafe.

"That's always the way with Kiduk," says Modiste's Marick Baars, who designed the airy, high-ceiling vastness that used to house a sawmill. It's now home to three stations in front of a modular frieze of glass, German oak, and stainless steel, a gridwork that divides the space with a bold minimalism reminiscent of Donald Judd.

"You don't see anything of the back bar. You don't see the dish washers. It's a bit different from the usual experience," Reus says.

"He's always eager to try something that's off the beaten path," says Baars, who also recently designed the chic Bonanza cafe in Mitte, resplendent with marble and polished stainless steel. One design of angular, futuristic lines, with a counter lifted on a cylinder that seems to float, presented challenges to plumbing and refrigeration.

"Bonanza is always a little bit under the magnifying glass with trends," Baars says, "and Kiduk wants to deliver on that."

But really what Reus was doing all along was bold but basic, intuitive.

"I did what everyone was talking about but not doing," Reus says, by which he means that he took the niche discoveries of home baristas and applied them in a commercial setting. And that has been the fulcrum for everything.

His origins, he says, "definitely helped me to keep the perspective very wide." With a father who worked for the government, he lived abroad frequently—in Australia and Hong Kong—and traveled extensively in the United States and Asia. But there's also a degree of personality.

"I'm always very curious," Reus says when I ask what made him the pioneer he was. "I just keep on going: I don't stop. I don't know why. I would say that I do see myself as uniquely obsessed."
—

Coffee Circle

Neighborhood Vibes

WORDS
Feride Yalav-Heckeroth

PHOTOGRAPHS
Ben Mönks

Pleasantly incongruous to the Wedding neighborhood's staunch social housing complexes bedecked in graffiti, Coffee Circle's flagship cafe is a sanctum of muted colors and comforting design details. Inside the quiet inner courtyard of a historic brick and stone structure from 1905, typical of Berlin's industrial architecture, the brand's first foray into the brick-and-mortar world of coffee was the realization of a longtime dream, as well as an experiment. "Coffee Circle was an online brand and we didn't have an offline identity, so this gave us a lot of freedom to explore," says Ersin Koray, the company's head of retail, "we created this cafe with our new vision, which then influenced and inspired the online brand, so that we changed it almost completely."

Founded in 2010 as an online coffee brand with a deep focus on social projects, Coffee Circle was awarded the Specialty Coffee Association Sustainability Award in 2022 for its biodiversity project in Ethiopia. Its Wedding location is also home to its own roastery, which opened in 2016, effectively altering its surroundings through the fragrance of freshly roasted coffee, sourced fairly and with positive impact. Located in a neighborhood on the brink of change, the company's first cafe is one of the few representatives of a new wave of young creatives, who have made Wedding their new base, sipping their Coffee Circle espresso shots from Brazilian Cerrado or a batch brew from Ethiopian Limu.

Just a few steps away, past the *döner* joints around Netellbeckplatz, the Michelin-starred restaurant Ernst hides behind an unassuming façade. Reservations are scarce for those who want to taste chef Dylan Watson-Brawn's cooking, inspired by his formative years in Japan. Across the street, Ernst's sister venue Julius is more casual, even open during the day for a cup of coffee roasted in-house over a fire and brewed by hand for each order. Another important piece of Wedding's new outlook is the Silent Green Cultural Quarter, a cultural center inside of a former crematorium, with its own cafe and a full roster of events.

Unlike its location in Wedding, Coffee Circle's second cafe in Mitte is a bit more confluent with the stylish ethos of its neighborhood. Close to the iconic Babylon Cinema, designed by Hans Poelzig in the 1920s, and the equally iconic Volksbühne theater, the Mitte branch's chic interior includes marble floors and a floral installation by the master florist Carolin Ruggaber. "Mitte is international, it gives you recognition in the tourist guides and the international coffee community," says Koray, "there is competition in the area so this was an experiment to see how strong the brand is and how much of an attraction we can create." Located on a quieter thoroughfare, away from the busier central shopping streets, Coffee Circle Mitte's neighbors include Luiban, a fine paper and stationery boutique, and Remi, a contemporary eatery with a seasonal and regional focus from the chefs of the well-known Lode & Stijn in Kreuzberg.

Far away from the international crowd, Coffee Circle's third branch is its most humble, a small cafe on a quiet street in the residential Bergmannkiez, where other coffee spots such as Chapter One and Two Trick Pony are frequented by young families, strollers in tow. Original tile work in forest-green decorates the floors of this kiosk-like coffee shop, where locals often stop by for a quick cup of coffee or to purchase coffee beans that they can brew at home. In fact, if there is one element that unites all of Coffee Circle's cafes, which seem to exhibit small differences inspired by their locations, it is the company's iconic color-coded coffee bags. A visual reminder of the brand's inception as an online store, a dedication to ending economic inequality in the coffee farming industry and a passion for bringing the most intricate of roasts from the remotest of locations.

—

Yoshimi Novailles, Coffee Circle

Ersin Koray, Coffee Circle

Zooming In on Neukölln

WORDS
Eve Hill-Agnus

PHOTOGRAPHS
Jack Hare

Long before I stayed there, I had heard of Neukölln on the South side of Berlin. David Bowie and Brian Eno immortalized the iconic neighborhood in their haunting, ambient 1977 piece swirling synthesizer with saxophone. Once gritty, this was a place of indie movie theaters and Turkish döner kebab sellers.

But from the first oat milk flat white, delivered on a wooden window sill in a smooth, glass tumbler, entrusted to me on deposit, I knew the Neukölln of my visit was more than a haven of culture and indie art. Rixbox Espresso, a tiny stand-alone cafe that juts into the Alfred-Scholz-Platz near the youth hostel where I slept, was an emblem of a newer Berlin, where ecology as well as expression were on the mind.

I returned day after day. Not surprisingly, looking deeper, I began noticing a rejection of waste in the local coffee culture. Passionate cafe owners impressed me, espousing notions that might seem radical but fit in organically here. If there is anything counter-cultural about this place, it's a counter-culture of sustainability.

"Regarding our deposit system, in the last three years, a thought process has been initiated to see how we can avoid as much waste as possible," Rixbox's owner Hossein Eggebrecht wrote to me later, "since the consumer culture of the last few decades has led us to an insane waste of packaging." Rixbox's milk is delivered in cleverly designed plastic containers, which are reusable and refillable, by a local dairy farm. He also serves all of his drinks in reusable vessels on a deposit basis. Customers get their deposit back when they return the vessel, reducing 40% of the packaging refuse. "Of course we will continue this process," he added. "A dream would be a zero-waste process."

Likewise, Isla Coffee is a bastion of mindful sustainability. American expat Peter Duran created this light-filled oasis six years ago. Here, the ricotta for French toast is made from

Steve Morris, Oslo Kaffebar

Steve Morris, Oslo Kaffebar

Peter Duran, Isla Coffee

leftover steamed milk, and a sprinkle of leek ash brings depth to a dish on the vegetarian (and mostly vegan) seasonal menu.

When Duran thinks about the components of his business, he considers the environmental, sustainable building blocks in a broad sense: How are employees paid? Can you reduce packaging? Are ingredients seasonal? Can you shorten the distance to good coffee? "I think that's really important, starting with the raw materials," he says.

Assuredly, you could say it's because he studied international relations with a sustainability focus and then earned a masters degree in sustainable development in food systems in the Netherlands, studying circular economies, wage structures, and sustainable food production on an industrial scale. And for him, the cafe was an experiment in best practices.

"We have a brilliant kitchen team. They are really systematic about how they use things," he says. "We throw away such little food compared to a lot of places."

Duran is kindred, in many ways, to Steve Morris, who is also an expat and co-owns Oslo Kaffebar. In 2011, Morris moved to Berlin from Scotland with his brother, both musicians lured by the German capital's music scene. He found his way as a barista because he could secure a visa that way.

Something else Duran and Morris share is their support of Kaffeeform, the company launched by Berlin native Julian Nachtigall-Lechner, a product designer who developed an ingenious process: he uses recycled coffee grounds and renewable raw materials to make a sparkly, wood-toned vessel—a coffee cup made of grounds. A bicycle courier "collective" picks up the grounds from coffee shops and roasters around Berlin.

For Morris, using Kaffeeform made sense. He replaced the porcelain cups behind the bar with Nachtigall-Lechner's speckled, umber-toned ones and found them to be practically indestructible. Initially, he wanted to craft the counter out of Kaffeeform ("because it's basically an infinite supply" and fully circular and sustainable) and ideally would outfit the quaint vinyl record shop in the back of the coffee shop with Kaffeeform shelves that complement the aesthetic of concrete and rough-hewn wood (his co-owner is Norwegian, and the inspiration is part cabin-in-the-woods).

The shift took some customers by surprise, as the texture and weight of the cup is not the now-ubiquitous third wave shop's luxurious ceramic or glass but closer to plastic. But it represented a staunch ideological commitment. "We really had to communicate to our customers why we were doing it. Ultimately, that was fun as well," Morris says, "because they were really happy to hear about it. I was humbled by how quickly they adapted."

Such is the face of progressive coffee. The goal remains "to avoid as much damage to the planet as possible," Morris says. And to do so by multifaceted means, whether fashioning a tight menu for zero waste or incentivizing customers who find creative ways to tote away multiple reusable to-go cups in a whimsical milk crate set-up, as Duran has been delighted to see some do at Isla.

"Coffee is the second most frequently traded good on the world market," Duran points out. "If we can shape everything around this drink that people enjoy on a daily basis," he sees Isla, for its part, as acting in "more of the soft power way. Other cafes look at us as an example. It's very much an emotional reaction right now in Germany: people just don't want anything to land in the garbage."

It's not an easy dance, however. Duran discusses frustrating nuances. "In Germany, when you serve cow's milk to-go, it's taxed at seven percent [European Value-Added Tax, or VAT, is usually already included in the listed price]," he explains. "But plant milk gets taxed 19% in-house or to-go." So, when 70% of the carbon footprint in a cappuccino is cow's milk, serving oat milk at the same price as cow's milk, as many cafes in Berlin do, is a question of political will.

In the culturally liberal capital, though, these ideas find a home. "Berlin's demographic has changed so much," Duran says. He's seen a shift in the last three or four of his eight years in the city. "Berlin in many ways is not Germany. I think it's the vegan capital of Europe, in a pure, per-capita sense." And, he emphasizes, "it's a place where it's easy to try out ideas."

Like any underground scene, the ecologically minded have found a place where their notions can thrive. They're thinking about circularity, and reaching for things that have an infinite supply, re-establishing where concern for the planet begins and ends—not stopping their efforts at the bean itself, but creating an envelope around it. Their commitment feels like a light, bright pulse.

Berlin can be a hard place, a brutalist place, Duran tells me, but also a place where you can take risks and not be afraid to fail. The fact that Berlin gives him that freedom feels like the future.

—

Coffee with Personality

WORDS
Austin Langlois

PHOTOGRAPHS
Magnus Pettersson

With its sprawling cityscape and expansive network of eclectic neighborhoods, Berlin is an easy city in which to get lost, architecturally and literally. Berlin stands apart from other prominent European destinations like Amsterdam, Lisbon, Rome, and Prague, because, after World War II, much of the city had been bombed and needed to be rebuilt. The remaining buildings were also pulled down and replaced over the following 70 years.

In contrast, when you walk around Amsterdam's canal district, which dates to the 17th century, many cobblestone streets and brick buildings wear the weathering of time and history. Same with Rome, where you can escape the harsh summer sun by standing in the shadow of ancient monuments that date back to the 7th century BCE.

The Berlin that today stands on the banks of the Spree River has become one of the most design-forward capitals of Europe, with bold, modernist architectural façades opposed by restored neo-classical landmarks and somber memorials. Every neighborhood has its own flavor, from the bohemian, artsy Kreuzberg to the restored, more-residential Prenzlauer Bern—making even short cross-city trips feel like an adventure.

***

The specialty coffee cafe design in Berlin takes after the rest of the city, shaking off the old industrial look that has become almost cliché in craft coffee (think the exposed brick and leather motifs of Devoción in Brooklyn, New York City, or the exposed beams and raw metal accents of Sightglass Coffee in the Mission District of San Francisco). Instead, many have embraced a more modern, minimalist aesthetic.

"Based on some of the most design-forward, prominent Berlin cafes, they don't follow the former trend of old wood and lamps from factories anymore to show the craft of specialty coffee," said Thorsten Keller, the owner of Hamburg-based online magazine shop Coffee Table Mags. "Instead, there has been a design shift for most of the new coffee places. They look modern, clean and somehow fancy, showing that specialty coffee is becoming more of a luxury product."

One example of this more upscale design shift is the Aussie-style cafe Zacharias Kaffeebar, which took on a quite quintessential European cafe look. Center stage in the room is an expansive, smooth walnut and opulent marble-surfaced coffee bar and a dark leather sofa meanders along one side. On sunny days, it's delightful to bask in front of the big, floor-to-ceiling windows sipping a "Magic"—a coffee drink exported from Melbourne (double ristretto topped with steamed milk).

"We took inspiration from the way traditional standing cafes in Italy engage with their customers, with a faster pace around the counter, which is designed to encourage guests to have a drink there and interact with the barista," said Zacharias Kaffeebar Co-Founder Johannes Knoetig. "On the other hand, the slower and more relaxed sitting area allows for longer stays, so we can tailor to the different needs of our customers."

Keller's favorite cafe design, Bonanza Coffee's Adalbertstrasse location, charted a different course on its minimalist design journey, with its lofty space outlined in modern and clean straight lines of glass and wood. The simple architecture is broken up by big leafy monsteras, transforming what would be a stark space into a cozy hideaway.

Jules

Akkurat Café

Danny Heyes, Akkurat Café

Luke O'Connor, Zacharias Kaffeebar

Zacharias Kaffeebar

"It allows you to hide or feel separated from the rest of the visitors when you just want to have an intimate talk with a good friend," said Keller. "It's also lovely that the roastery is in a backyard, so you can also relax in front of the roastery on summer days without the noise and distractions from the big city."

Munich-based roastery Man versus Machine takes minimalism and luxury to a whole new level with their counter-service cafe in a Lacoste boutique. Bathed in alligator-green, the simple, walk-up window displays only a La Marzocco espresso machine and a tray of croissants and *pain au chocolat*.

Meanwhile, other cafes have taken a less branded, more localized approach, like Jules, with two distinct locations: a high-fashion cafe in Geisberg and a more industrial, casual cafe-biergarten in Kreuzberg. Similarly, Five Elephant Roastery runs four locations across the city, using unique materials and distinctive designs to match the vibe of each of the cafes' neighborhoods. For example, its city-center spot in the Mitte district shows off with glossy, black-tiled wainscoting juxtaposed with whitewashed walls and crisp fluorescent lights. Meanwhile, its location in the famous KaDeWe department store, dial up the design with a bold terrazzo-flanked bar and matching ink-black machines. And as a foil to the others, the more hipster Kreuzberg cafe takes a softer, more organic turn, swathed in soft wood with big windows bringing in the warmth of the tree-lined street outside.

For Berlin coffee roasters, attention to design doesn't just stop at the physical space; they're also well-known for their artistic approach to coffee bean packaging as well. Here, the roasters seem to have landed in two different camps, opting for either simple and minimalist or colorful and bold.

The established specialty coffee strongholds, known as the 'Big Three,' (THE BARN, and the aforementioned Bonanza Coffee Roasters and Five Elephant) were some of the first to the craft coffee scene, and have since become well-known across the world. Their aesthetic relies heavily on their logo, use of white space and simple typography to carry the packaging. Five Elephant dials up its design language by wrapping its white bags in a bright, color-blocked sleeve, with its elephant logo displayed prominently on top.

For August63, a newer roaster that opened in September of 2021, Founder Ken Braz and Head of Design Carla Blaumann knew they needed a more "eye-catching" design to compete.

"We had to create something new in order to stand out in the very dense landscape of Berlin coffee roasters," said Blaumann. "[As such], we developed a basic structure that served as a canvas for a unique design, which would capture consumers' attention, while also preserving the brand's recognition value," said Blaumann.

The framed label on the front is divided into two sections. The left side displays a unique illustration (often a collage) that's inspired both by the heritage of the coffee as well as its unique flavor profiles, while the right side includes the sourcing details and tasting notes.

"Each of our designs represents the unique qualities of the coffee," said Blaumann. "Some are inspired by the farm where the coffee was grown, while others reflect the environment and "mood" where the coffee will be enjoyed or the complexity of the flavor profile. We also collaborate with other designers, who create their own unique designs for our coffee bags.

As to the color palette of each of the playful designs, each is linked to the specific coffee.

"While tasting coffees on the cupping table, I can usually link flavors with colors, which helps me understand the different taste nuances," said Braz. "That's why each coffee has different color schemes in order for the consumer to understand the taste notes better."

***

For the eighth-most popular city destination in the world, it's surprising that Berlin's coffee scene remains decidedly local. It's not a city that wears its coffee culture on its chest; instead, it's like a treasure hunt, with hidden gems strewn across its 12 distinct districts. And while it may not get the same attention of more popular craft coffee destinations like Copenhagen, Tokyo, or San Francisco, it has taken the art of the full consumer experience to a totally different level—underscoring that what's outside the cup is equally important as what's inside.
—

The New Bakers of Berlin

WORDS
J.R.M. Owens

PHOTOGRAPHS
Franz Grünewald and Noel Richter

Across the tatters of the Iron Curtain there is today in Germany's capital a renaissance in baking. Like the baristas who led the third wave of coffee here, the new bakers in Berlin are mainly outsiders by birth. And their work, like art, is for its own sake.

East meets West: Berlin's baking tradition

Draw a map of northern Europe and of eastern Europe and the two borders will intersect around Berlin. Situated as the major city on the North European Plain, Berlin also marks the frontier of the old Soviet Union. Against this backdrop, the bakers of Berlin have begun their work.

In her 2022 book "New European Baking," Laurel Kratochvila provides 99 original recipes through the stories of 11 bakers from Madrid to Warsaw at the forefront of this wave of "new baking." A Jewish-American from New England, Kratochvila married a Czech man (with whom she opened a bookstore in Berlin). Since creating Fine Bagels in 2012, she has been at the vanguard of Berlin's new bakers.

"The 20th century was generally a bad time for European bakeries," she writes. "Two world wars and an Iron Curtain didn't help the situation. But industrialization, more than anything, was to blame. Technology changed everything about [baking]." Across Europe this new approach to baking is marked by a return to the pre-industrialized earth and the food that it produced, and it's on display best where East meets West: Berlin.

"Berlin is in the old East of Germany, and it is still quite affected by that," says Luke Smetham, founder of Albatross Bakery in the Berlin neighborhood of Kreuzberg. "As a result of the war and the old split, most of the flour and most of everything you can find is quite industrialized."

The area around Berlin and north to the coast "used to be the grain belt for all of Prussia and a lot of Europe," he says, "where there's a lot of [grain] varieties grown and a lot of small craft mills. [But] when there was East Germany and the Russians, they shut down all these mills because it wasn't efficient."

North of the Danube River is historically the domain of rye, according to Frithjof Wodarg, co-founder of Gorilla Bäckerei, a bakery with locations in Berlin's Schöneberg and Neukölln neighborhoods. "If you were growing wheat farther in the north, you just didn't get enough yield out of it," he says. "Obviously this all changed with the further industrialization of agriculture: you sort of planted whatever you wanted anywhere."

"If your geography allows you to grow these kinds of wheat," Wodarg says, "then you have a food culture that grows out of that. "Lighter, whiter [bread] is something that you didn't have in the northern parts of Germany or Europe for that matter. It was darker, denser [bread]."

The dark, dense bread produced its own food culture. The German word for dinner, *abendbrot*, translates literally as "evening bread." Germans traditionally "eat the bigger, warm meal at lunch, and then in the evenings you have bread with stuff," Wodarg says. He contrasts this with the French relationship to bread: "French people eat bread as a side to sort of dip their sauce, or a sandwich, but it's not like you have a meal centered around bread. And that's something that is very traditionally German, for which we would [also have] rye bread…it's more substantial bread, and there's just more calories."

Twentieth century Berlin stood in the crosswinds of industry and war. These destroyed the local grain culture, and they commodified German baking tradition. Into this came the worldwide coffee revolution in the early years of the twenty-first century. The new bakers followed shortly after, a motley group of outsiders who are revitalizing the Berlin baking scene.

"Bread has the power to connect the people to the city": Berlin's new bakers

In Berlin the new bakers followed the new baristas. First came coffee: Bonanza Coffee Roasters opened in 2006, followed in 2010 by Five Elephant and THE BARN. Then came the bakers: Kratochvila's Fine Bagels began in 2012; Albatross Bakery would not open as Berlin's first major sourdough endeavor until 2017, followed in 2019 by KEIT, a bakery with two locations, and in 2020 by Gorilla Bäckerei.

Cory Andreen, an American who's been at the forefront of the Berlin coffee scene since its beginning, describes the overlapping appeal of specialty coffee with new baking, natural wines, and craft beer. "Almost worldwide you saw these kinds of waves happening over the past couple of decades," Andreen says. "Anyone who is involved with one of those things individually, if they don't have exposure to anything else, like good baked goods…it [doesn't] take long before they get kind of initiated into that wider world. I think more and more people are seeing the crossover."

KEIT

Fabian Müller, Gorilla Bäckerei

Linnea Riensberg & Georgina Miller, Gorilla Bäckerei

Fabian Müller, Gorilla Bäckerei

Frithjof Wodarg & Matteo Angioi Petia, Gorilla Bäckerei

Geoff Stewart, Anders Alkaersig, Jasmin Lünstroth, & Luke Smetham, Albatross Bakery

That crossover broadens horizons and it also brings into focus one's own specialty. Andreen's latest project is Motel Minibar, a coffee and beer canning business that took many cues from the well-honed practice of beer canning. "For me, when I started getting into tasting beer and coffee, different stuff, it was also about trying to be better at my job in coffee," he says. "I wanted to better understand different processes of fermentation. I wanted to also explore some flavor profiles that you can't get in coffee; for all the breadth and depth that you get in coffee, obviously there's a bunch of stuff that you don't get."

Berlin has one of the world's highest density of organic markets per capita, and when specialty coffee came into the city, natural fermentation found a conducive climate. And it grew.

From the the United States, Denmark, The United Kingdom, and Australia came the new bakers. While Berlin's established baking tradition was preserved by Germans, its new baking scene is dominated by newcomers. "It is mostly expats," says Smetham, an Englishman by way of Australia. "I think it's the same anywhere—if you're an immigrant and you move, then you work in entry or low-level jobs. It could either be making a restaurant of your country's cuisine… speciality coffee in this case."

The new bakers came at a time when Berlin changed also in other ways. The city has become a tech hub: the 2010s saw giants like Amazon and Microsoft open offices, along with hundreds of startups fueled by 150% investment growth year over year since 2017.

Since 2010, the "perspective and the attitude of the city" has changed, says Wodarg, who is a Berliner by birth, noting that it's now "an international [metropolis], and not just a German city." Berlin has become "a more international, more curious city—in a culinary way more curious, and also a bit more ambitious."

More importantly, Berlin's international appetite is hungry for something new. "It's not just a thing about the bakeries being there or not," Wodarg says. "The city has changed so much: the audience has changed, your customers have changed; there's more of a willingness to pay for good quality."

"It would have been difficult to have a bakery like ours 20 years ago in Berlin," he says. "Now there is a much larger part of the population [that is] willing to pay for high quality food, even if they are not super rich." Smetham agrees: "The market is starting to develop."

KEIT has taken a unique approach to supplying that market: with a startup mentality. A collaboration between former Adidas coworkers Thanos Petalotis and Kolja Orzeszko, KEIT began by conducting man-on-the-street interviews to understand Berliners' relationship to bread. Their survey suggested that the relationship was "broken," Orzeszko says,—because through industrialization "bread became such a big commodity," which led to subpar standards and ill health effects.

"We set ourselves a radius of 100 kilometers around Berlin, where we said: Everything we source ideally comes from within these 100 kilometers," Orzeszko says. "Bread has the power to connect the people to the city. If you source flour from Scandinavia or from Italy or whatever, everyone can get a really good flour. Obviously it still takes craftsmanship to [make] nice bread, but what truly connects people to a city and what you can only get here and what makes it unique is if you only get ingredients from Berlin."

This emphasis on local sourcing has required numerous trips to farmers and millers in the surrounding area, negotiating what kinds of wheat to plant in order to have grain for the following year. "Since we wanted to be local," Orzeszko says, "we knew that we have to have the conversation with farmers and we wanted to have an impact also on Berlin, so it's not a one-way street… it's [about] how can we work together to get you where we, as a partnership, then need to be. And with a feedback loop as drawn-out as a wheat harvest, it [has] taken years to expand. KEIT began by serving one kind of loaf only, and even now its menu is just five different loaves.

Recently, KEIT fully realized its goal of being 100% local. "In the beginning it was like a two percent compromise that we had in our bread," Orzeszko explains, because they sourced the dough's salt from abroad. But driven to meet the goal set out from their market research, they combed through university studies to discover Berlin-area salt production sites from the medieval age. They struck a deal with a local thermal bath which uses its own salt in therapeutic applications, making KEIT "the only business—not just bakery—that gets salt locally from Berlin… Now the bread is 100% local."

One of the most established personalities in the Berlin baking scene is Kratochvila, whose Fine Bagels started on a $300 budget in a converted closet. She began making small batches of bagels, and in so doing she brought bagels full circle: From their likely origin in 17th century Krakow, the bagel traveled in Jewish recipe books to New York. With Fine Bagels now a smooth operation she has gone on to publish her own cookbook and to open a natural wine bar, Le Balto.

The presence of a Jewish bakery in Berlin has proven irresistible for many journalists. But the true story is more simple and more elegant than some suppose. "For me, it's not about bringing a Jewish product to Berlin but bringing a wonderful food that I hate seeing misrepresented," Kratochvila says. "It seems that the Berlin definition of a bagel is a bread roll with a hole in the middle, whereas a bagel is a lot more than that. I was unable to find one to my satisfaction in this city, so I started doing them myself." The existence of a Jewish bakery in Berlin is coincidence. It is not meant as a statement, it is too self-forgetting for that; it is a love.

Smetham parallels what's happening in baking to what has happened in coffee: "A lot of specialty coffee did kind of start as an Australian thing," and in centuries past, coffee "came from all the Italian immigrants," he says. "Something from one culture comes to another, gets tweaked, gets kind of doctored up, gets experimented and played with—we're a bit less respectful of some traditions in a way—and then it gets moved again where someone else… plays around with it."

The new bakers of Berlin have come by many ways to a city once rich in its baking tradition. They are making it so again, taking what they know and what they find and being a bit less respectful of some traditions than others might like. In the small hours of the morning across Berlin bakers rise to their craft, as Kratochvila says: "Because I needed something for myself!"

—

Enjoying a Cup of עוואָק in Berlin

WORDS
Jonathan Shipley

PHOTOGRAPHS
Fabian Schmid

Amidst thousands of works of art at the Jewish Museum in the Kreuzberg district: coffee. Amidst old photographs and musty volumes of Jewish lore: coffee. Amidst the personal histories of Jews collected there, coffee is being served at Café Lina.

The cafe is abuzz with activity. It's a place for conversation over labneh; reflection over sesame rings; thoughtful dialogue over latkes and baklava; cakes and coffee.

When visitors finish their small repasts at Café Lina, perhaps they'll continue their exploration of the museum's vast holdings. Perhaps they'll walk outside, not far from Checkpoint Charlie and the former Berlin Wall, to wander Berlin's warren of busy, city streets. Vivified by the Jewish Museum, and the coffee served therein, they add their own thrum to Berlin's beating heart. Perhaps they have some understanding that coffee made its way to that particular Jewish cafe, in that particular Jewish museum, because of Jews.

To know how coffee got into a Café Lina cup in downtown Berlin in 2023, one has to go back in time and travel far distances. The time was the 9th century and the place was the city of Kafia in Ethiopia. It was there that coffee sprung forth.

From Africa, coffee extended across the Ottoman Empire, where people across a wide range of religious affiliations—Muslim, Christian, Jew—drank coffee to stay alert during their morning and evening devotions.

The drink sparked creativity and thought. Among the Jewish populations, it also sparked questions. Was coffee kosher? Yes. Was coffee a medicine? No. Should there be a blessing said before coffee is consumed? Yes. *Shehakol* was the blessing one used before imbibing most any food or drink.

As coffee's popularity grew, its importance was reinforced. By the 16th century, coffee houses began to spring up, from Constantinople and Damascus to Cairo and Mecca.

A botanist named Leonhard Rouwolf introduced coffee to Germans in 1573. He was the first European to mention coffee and the first to mention the beverage in print.

Not only a botanist, Rouwolf was also the official physician to the town of Augsburg, one of Germany's oldest cities, situated in Bavaria. He wrote, "…they have a very good drink, by them called Chaube that is almost as black as ink, and very good in illness, chiefly that of the stomach; of this they drink in the morning early in open places before everybody." He continued, "without any fear or regard, out of China cups, as hot as they can."

Germany's coffee culture started beating for the first time with Rouwolf's recommendations. Neighboring countries also looked upon coffee positively, and coffee's growth in Europe was, in part, because of the work of Jews.

During the Enlightenment, Jews were being welcomed into many European societies, which considered coffee a drink for the wealthy and well heeled. And Jewish merchants and Jewish leaders in these communities, eager to emulate their non-Jewish counterparts, began to champion coffee far and wide.

The Jews enjoyed coffee, and appreciated its benefits, both economically and physically. It could affect one's mood profoundly. "One cannot attain presence of mind without the aid of coffee," said Hezekiah da Silva, an Italian rabbi in the late 1600s.

In fact, the first coffeehouse in Europe opened in Livorno, Italy in 1632 by a

Jewish Museum

THE BARN—Cafe Kranzler

Café Lina, Jewish Museum

Jewish merchant. And in 1650, England's first coffee house opened, also by a Jew. Called the Angel Inn, it was owned and operated by a Lebanese man known locally as Jacob the Jew.

But it took some time for the coffeehouse to take hold in Berlin, then capital to the kingdom of Prussia. This was partially due to the opposition of the coffee industry by the Prussian crown.

"My people must drink beer," proclaimed by the Prussian king, Frederick the Great. And at his direction, authorities began clamping down on the coffee trade. Restrictions were put in place and then more restrictions on top of that. The fear was that the burgeoning coffee industry would be detrimental to Prussia's booming beer industry.

Although coffee's heartbeat was diminished in Prussia, it would not be quieted. People could, and wanted to drink both coffee and beer and so they did.

Meanwhile, coffeehouses in neighboring countries became hives for the local intelligentsia. In Austria, Vienna's coffeehouses became meeting houses for artists and intellectuals; politicians and businessmen. The same was happening in Budapest and elsewhere.

The Haskalah, the Jewish Enlightenment, was a small group of Jewish intellectuals in central and eastern Europe from the last decades of the 18th century until the end of the 19th century. Their meeting places: coffeehouses.

It was only a matter of time before the same would be true in Berlin.

"I must inform you of a new establishment that I founded here in Berlin," journalist Johann George Muchler wrote in a letter dated April of 1756. His Gelehrtes Kaffeehaus was "a society of forty people, mostly men of learning, but artists too… Members can go there every day." He wrote, "coffee and whatever one wants is to be had at a cheap price, and one meets pleasant company."

Berlin was thrumming with the clatter of coffee cups and the din of rich conversation in Muchler's coffeehouse and others in the city. By the 19th century, Berlin's Jewish coffeehouses were on the forefront of societal change, and became places where exchanges of thoughts and ideas happened.

As coffeehouses continued to blossom in Berlin for the wealthy and well-to-do, other establishments began forming for the commoner. The *cafe konditorei* (literally translated as "cafe confectionery") began to emerge in the city as another place for the Jewish people. It was for working classes. Socialist writer Ernst Dronke wrote that they were "the meeting place of the like-minded who speak out about their interests; they are a kind of club." He continued, "everyone who has any kind of interest at all in public life turns out in the *Cafe-Konditoreien*."

Berlin's Jews turned out to drink coffee and share ideas in places like Cafe Josty, Cafe Stehely, Cafe Kranzler, Cafe Monopol, Cafe Bauer, Cafe du Westens, and others. Through the political upheavals of the 19th century and onward, Berlin's Jewish community congregated where coffee was being served, building stronger communities by doing so.

Stillness, of course, came for Berlin's Jews with Hitler's rise to power. The Nazi regime all but destroyed Jewish culture. With it, the Jewish coffeehouses that were woven deeply into the collective identity of Berlin unraveled. In 1933, novelist Wolfgang Koeppen wrote of Berlin's once thriving and illustrious Romanisches Cafe, "We saw the terrace and cafe disappear… dissolve to nothing."

From nothing, something grew again. The Jewish people, their culture, and their coffee dissolved during the war, but was reimagined after. The Jewish Museum is a testament to what came before and what came after. The coffee brewed in Café Lina is a liquid tie that binds old and new; what was and what is; what has been and would could be. The life of botanist Leonhard Rouwolf isn't far from the lively Bäckerei Kädtler today, in the Prenzlauer Berg neighborhood. The work of Jacob the Jew isn't too distant from the work of a barista at today's Zeit für Brot, a trendy cafe near Olivaer Platz.

Germany has one of the fastest growing Jewish populations of any European country. Berlin has the largest Jewish community in Germany. The bagels are warm. The coffee is hot. The city's heart thrums.

—

Market Days

WORDS
Rachel Preece

PHOTOGRAPHS
Ben Mönks

Nineteenth century Berlin was beleaguered by cholera, typhoid, and diphtheria epidemics. Tuberculosis was rife—roughly a seventh of the German population died of the disease—and in the 1880s, a Berlin Exhibition of Hygiene was held, a desperate attempt to mitigate disease by educating citizens. Rudolf Virchow, social reformer and so-called "pope of medicine," set about improving city sanitation by moving markets indoors.

One of 14 covered markets in Berlin, Markthalle Neun opened in the district of Kreuzberg in 1891. It was one of the few that were not destroyed by bombing in the Second World War. While the building had remained largely intact, the infrastructure surrounding it had not. Kreuzberg became a disconnected hinterland, with almost half of the district's housing unusable.

The market was open, but barely. It continued to limp along, and renovation work in the early nineties wasn't enough to revive it. In 2011, three young Germans took over the market from the City of Berlin. Their ardor was galvanizing. Today, the market hall is synonymous with high-quality produce and culinary excellence. Vendors sell goods from Berlin and from across the world, reflecting Kreuzberg's cultural diversity.

Kaffee 9 launched in Markthalle Neun in 2012. "I was often in London for research purposes," founder Philipp Reichel tells me. "Borough Market and the Monmouth Coffee Company inspired us all at the market. They are the reason we were so keen to have a cafe and a roastery together." Reichel's roastery has a strong emphasis on equity, and releases annual transparency reports on coffee production costs. He founded the Berlin Coffee Festival in 2015 with a similar focus—putting the farmers in the limelight.

Paula Leu, Kaffee 9

Vanessa Schönfeld Janeva, Kaffee 9

Emine Koc, Kaffee 9

Kaffee 9 was one of the first vendors to join the market under its new management, and he looks back on those early days fondly: "Markthalle Neun shaped me as a person. The energy of being in a space with so many like-minded people and working together on making good food and drink was special. There was a never-ending, fascinating atmosphere of optimism. Due to its culture and its past, Germany does not have the most experienced culinary tongue. Good food was celebrated and communicated every day in Markthalle Neun." Matthias Becker opened the raw milk cheesemonger Alte Milch in the market in 2015. He says the same: "Being able to connect with all of these people that are passionate about flavors is extraordinary."

Markthalle Neun has influenced Kreuzberg's transformation over the past decade. It is a bohemian, multicultural neighborhood that has undergone hyper-gentrification. "In those early years, Kreuzberg was characterized by immigrants and old Kreuzbergers," Reichel says, "but that has changed, and Markthalle Neun unintentionally contributed to that." From 2012-2017, Berlin grew by almost a quarter million people. Four out of five were foreigners. It has been a mixed blessing for the neighborhood, frequently deemed "iconic" and "hip" by travel guides.

Duygu Uzuner grew up in Kreuzberg and runs a stall selling Turkish *manti* (tiny, savory stuffed dumplings) at Markthalle Neun. Over the years, she has seen her *kiez*, as Berliners fondly refer to their neighborhoods, change beyond measure. "When I was growing up, Kreuzberg was called a ghetto. People wanted to move out of the neighborhood. Now, everyone wants to live here and rents have skyrocketed. I love it here. There's a feeling of acceptance. No one is excluded because of how they look or for their religious beliefs."

Reichel's roastery Vote was a part of Kaffee 9 for five years. Requiring more space, Vote moved south to Neukölln in 2021. His second cafe, the no-waste cafe Isla Coffee, is midway between Markthalle Neun and Vote's new roastery. Now, the entire city is peppered with specialty coffee bars and Reichel believes that Germany's capital is the vanguard of the country's third wave coffee culture. "In Berlin in particular, specialty coffee has come a long way. Customers are willing to pay for good coffee. In other parts of Germany, it is more difficult. As in many other respects, Berlin is an exception."

—

Barista's Choice

WORDS
Imogen Lepere

PHOTOGRAPHS
Maria Louceiro

French and Italian styles have strutted at the front of Europe's high fashion scene for generations. But, as anyone interested in vintage clothes and limited edition sneakers knows, Berlin rules on the streets—and the eastern neighborhoods of Mitte, Neukölln, and Kreuzberg remain the nucleus of the city's underground scene.

This can largely be traced back to the Cold War, when the German Democratic Republic built the Berlin Wall to stop its population from fleeing Soviet-controlled East Berlin. By that point, so many people had left the eastern side of the city, young people from the West could volunteer to move there to avoid compulsory military service. As a result, East Berlin became a hotbed of liberal types who stayed on even after the wall was torn down in 1989 and founded the art, design, and music scenes that still thrive in these streets today. It's here you'll see club kids wearing tire-thick platform boots mixing with morning commuters on the train after a night at the popular music venue Berghain, artists with micro-fringes and dyed eyebrows sipping orange wine at Motif Wein and creatives who look like they've stepped out of a VICE documentary walking their dogs around Tempelhofer Feld.

Whether providing a space for makers to collaborate, or a quick caffeine-fix to get them through the day after a night spent dancing to techno, cafes are inextricably entwined with the creative scene in the neighborhoods that were formerly East Berlin. So who better to tell us where to shop for stylish clothes than the baristas at some of the most fashionable spots in the city?

Martina Bazzon & Shota Kabasawa, House of Small Wonders

Martina Bazzan & Shota Kabasawa, House of Small Wonders

Peter Duran, Isla Coffee

Jaques Lorenzen, Hallesches Haus

Hannes Haake, Distrikt
With its pavement tables and tiled floor, Distrikt is one of Mitte's most beloved and aesthetically pleasing cafes. It serves beans roasted by independent European operations including nearby roastery Fjord.

"Berlin´s fashion scene has an anarchist bent that matches the grit of the city. The mix of cultures and open mindedness allows Berliners to dress eclectically. But functionality is key—you'll rarely see anyone wearing anything they can't cycle home in. As a barista you're interacting with the city's residents and visitors in a unique way—you get to see people as they start their day or catch them in between activities so sometimes you notice their clothes and wonder what they do for work or where they're headed. Subconsciously, you're picking up on the latest fashion trends which might explain why so many baristas have great style.

I try not to take my clothes too seriously and mostly look for quality so I can get a lot of wear out of it. My style is sort of utilitarian, especially when I know I'll be working a coffee shift that tends to get quite messy.

At Distrikt, we've tried to cultivate a warm atmosphere by creating a cozy space and by focusing on offering friendly service, which was not the norm in Berlin, especially some years ago. However, within the industry there is a really strong sense of community. As an owner, I always feel I can reach out to other independent coffee shops and ask for advice in tough times."

Haake likes Voo, a fashion and design concept store with a great coffee shop inside. He also loves Another June Vintage, a cool vintage furniture store near Tempelhof Feld, and recommends Nella Beljan Gallery for its rotating selection of clothing and homewares from small brands and designers.

Christian Valentine Robinson, Annelies
Located opposite Gorlitzer Park in Kreuzberg, Annelies is the perfect spot for soaking in some afternoon sun, accompanied by single-origin coffee from La Cabra roastery in Denmark and delicious pastries from award-winning bakery Albatross.

"I would describe Berlin's fashion scene in one sentence as 'not afraid to just be'. Whether you want to express eccentricity or feel comfortable in basics, you can do and be whatever you want and continually experiment. Nobody will really question it as everyone is busy doing the same. Neutral tones and utility styles are big here, and both work well for being a barista. As much as I would love to work in [an] outrageous [outfit], you're constantly under threat of ruining your best garments with espresso stains.

The coffee scene in Berlin has definitely exploded and continues to grow. I sometimes worry it has become too 'sceney' but I enjoy the effort that is made to design spaces that really invite people in, allow for coworking as well as community and provide a sanctuary from the mayhem. At Annelies, we're right next to Gorlitzer Park. Facing southwest, we get the most glorious golden hours. Our menu features inventive twists on classic brunch staples while highlighting mindfully sourced, local ingredients."

Studio Li:ne is primarily a florist, Robinson notes, which specializes in more experimental flower arrangements. But she also likes it for the gorgeous homewares it sells by Berlin artists. She also likes Isla—a clothing boutique and nail salon in Mitte—for its community driven approach, as it regularly works with local designers to host special events that bring people together through fashion. For vintage clothing, Sing Blackbird is Robinson's go-to. "It is thoughtfully curated and offers top quality, and I fall in love with something on each visit. Last time, it was a pair of low-rise, white flares."

Peter Duran, Isla Coffee
A local hangout in Neukölln, petite Isla has a zen-like atmosphere thanks to handmade, Scandi-inspired furniture and a jungle of house plants. It strives to minimize waste through a plant-based menu and cups made from recycled coffee beans.

"Berlin's fashion scene is a perfect reflection of the city: wild, varied, do-what-you-want-because-no-one-cares. I think people that work in coffee and fashion choose what they consume with more intention than most. We identify deeply with the choices we make.

Just like its fashion scene, Berlin's specialty coffee [scene] is incredibly diverse and finds itself in a pretty interesting phase. The focus is how to become better at being a good host and making what we love, namely coffee, more accessible to the general public. In the past (I've been in coffee here for nine years), specialty coffee felt like either something for the rich, hipster expats, or tourists. But, as the city has developed, so has its approach to specialty coffee. It's now fully integrated into Berlin's hospitality scene and has become a part of more people's daily lives.

Obviously, we think our coffee is great and try hard to make sure we're serving the best brews this side of town. But we think that 80% of the specialty coffee experience is everything other than the drink. A friendly team, good vibe, and strong values are what keep people coming back. We're one of the first low-waste, circular economy-focused cafes in Europe and definitely the first in Berlin."

Duran likes to shop at Shio, which he says is "one of the first places in Berlin to offer upcycled clothing that is truly beautiful and unique." He notes that "Kate [Pinkstone], the owner, made our aprons and cushions [at Isla Coffee] as well."

Loppis Vintage is near one of Duran's favorite cafes, Companion. The owner, he says, always has nice, everyday stuff that you won't see in other vintage shops in Berlin. And Side by Side, which is near Isla Coffee, sells vintage clothing that Duran says is "either slightly ahead of the curve or totally timeless, like the Wrangler black corduroy shirt I recently picked up there."

Martina Bazzan, House of Small Wonder
Berlin meets Japan at this eclectic eatery on Auguststrasse in Mitte. Expect a leafy courtyard, oriental rugs offset by statement wallpaper, and a brunch menu laced with Asian flavors such as miso, yuzu, and matcha.

"Making coffee is like making art [because] it's an expression of self—as is fashion. Baristas are all a bit quirky in their own way and fashion is the best tool to show off their unique personalities. I would describe my look as diverse, bold, and dashing, all adjectives that could be used for Berlin's fashion scene in general.

The city is exploding with specialty coffee options, but I think the best coffee in town is definitely from THE BARN—I'm not usually a big fan of filtered coffee, but what I get there is fantastic. We use beans from Bonanza and the aroma is incredible. The genuine welcome of the team can be felt as soon as you open the door."

Hannes Haake, Distrikt

Christian Valentine Robinson, Annelies

"PLATTE.Berlin is more like an art space because it hosts exhibitions about sustainability as well as exceptional pieces by emerging designers," Bazzan says. She loves that it transforms fashion into an experience where you can learn to buy in a way that protects the planet. HahaYoureUgly is her all-time favorite second-hand shop. "It has an incredible selection of vintage clothes and reworked pieces. Last time I was there, I got an incredible oversized jacket." And Bazzan says that Juno Juno is "a real gem for one-of-a-kind designer pieces that are fabulous and unique." She says she made her favorite purchase here: the ultimate cowboy boots that she can't stop wearing.

Shota Kabasawa, House of Small Wonders
"Berlin's fashion scene is so hugely varied it's almost impossible to describe and barista style is a microcosm of that. Coffee, culture, and fashion have coexisted for a long time and baristas meet people from many different countries every day, so no two ever have the same look.

Similarly, Berlin has a wide range of specialty coffee shops large and small, where you can experience the tastes of different beans and roasting methods from lots of countries. One of the things that makes House of Small Wonders unique is that it serves a Japanese brunch and features fusion drinks such as matcha lattes and yuzu sours."

Burg & Schild is Kabasawa's top pick for good-quality, Japanese denim and leather jackets. He also likes Repeater for its large selection of American vintage clothing, which he notes is great for comfy casuals. Kabasawa also says that Soultrade Recordstore has a great selection of soul, jazz, and funk. Last time he visited, he picked up a copy of "Dreams of a Love Supreme" by Wendell Harrison.

—

Douglas C 47 Candy Bomber

Operation Santa Claus

WORDS & PHOTOGRAPHS
Christian Eschner

For years, Harmen de Keijzer has tried to find a home inside the abandoned buildings on the northern side of Airport Tempelhof. During the Cold War, these parts were used as a U.S. Air Force officers hotel. In between flights, officers hung out at the hotel bar, where they were provided snacks, enjoyed jazz music, and had hot coffee while admiring Tempelhof's neo-classical elegance. De Keijzer opened Orville's inside the former officers bar as a lunch cafe, Friday night jazz bar, and event space. Just like in the old days, Orville's serves hot drinks and snacks reminiscent of that Cold War era.

However, the more you walk towards the former Airport Tempelhof, towards its monumental structures, the less you would expect to find a cafe. Tempelhof's curved, semicircular main building is supposed to evoke an eagle in flight. Punctuated by towers like fortifications, its thin rectangular windows carry the walls of the terminal halls elegantly and lightly. The emptiness of the space however weighs heavily on visitors who dare to have a look inside Tempelhof, which was designed under the direction of head Nazi architect Albert Speer. It was intended as the perfect portal to Adolf Hitler's plan of a redesigned Berlin. The loneliness of the 300-foot plaza, Eagle Square, which served as a grand entrance to the airport, is now interrupted only by the presence of Berlin's police headquarters in the southern flank of buildings.

Yet, Tempelhof would acquire its true fame and aura after Hitler's downfall.

In the aftermath of WWII, the eastern half of Germany was occupied by the Soviet Union, while the western half of Germany was occupied by the Allies—the Americans, British, and French troops. It was decided to not only split Germany into occupied zones but also to divide Berlin, a city deeply embedded within Soviet-occupied Germany. The western half of the city was carved into three Allied-occupied zones, and the eastern side of the city was occupied by the Soviets.

In Soviet-occupied East Berlin, the Soviet leader Joseph Stalin swiftly unified political parties to create the German Communist Party. However, Berliners, hostile to their Russian occupiers, overwhelmingly voted for the Social Democratic candidate Ernst Reuter as their mayor. In 1948, Reuter gave a memorable speech in front of the shattered Reichstags building to a crowd of almost half a million. He appealed to the people of this world never to abandon the city of Berlin and its inhabitants.

The Soviet Union then stripped East Berlin of factories, technicians, and wealth as war reparations. Stalin further hoped to put enough pressure on the Allies to give up their part of Berlin altogether by restricting military and civilian traffic from West Germany to Berlin, hoping to choke off the Allied island foothold within Soviet-controlled Germany.

After the introduction of a West German currency, Stalin stepped up his game of deterrence. He cut all land and water connections to West Berlin, and eventually stopped Soviet food and energy supplies altogether, bringing West Berlin to the verge of a humanitarian catastrophe. When the blockade began, the people of West Berlin had about 30 days of stock left. Unlike the ground routes to Berlin, the three air corridors had to remain open by treaty and could only be used by unarmed aircraft. But could a city of such a scale be provided enough supply by airfreight alone? In order to prevent a population of two million from

starving, by calculation of the British Air Commodore, West Berlin would need 1,534 tons of foodstuff every single day and twice that daily tonnage of coal to survive the winter months. This did not seem to be a feasible task considering the fact that planes at that time only had an average payload of around five tons per flight.

Ultimately, President Harry S. Truman determined that it was of utmost importance that the United States remain a presence in West Berlin, committing to airlifts to Tempelhof to supply West Berlin with the provisions it needed. To run this operation—now known as the Berlin Airlift—as efficiently as possible, pilots had to take three flights a day, with airlift flights every four minutes. There were as many as 1,440 landings daily. This traffic brought a lot of jobs to Tempelhof, including staffing food trucks next to the runway to distribute food and hot coffee for crew and pilots working around the clock. After years of running into air raid shelters away from bombers, Berliners were now running towards incoming aircraft. Instead of being abandoned, they were supplied life-sustaining provisions and with a renewed sense of friendship.

To prop up morale during the harsh winter months of 1948-1949, operation Santa Claus was started. Over 11 tons of coffee were flown into Tempelhof, and, perhaps more memorably, some pilots started dropping chocolate bars attached to little homemade parachutes to German children. Gail Halvorsen was the first pilot to do so, which earned him the nickname "The Berlin Candy Bomber." When he'd wiggle the wings of his airplane, the kids knew it was him.

After 11 months of these airlifts, the Soviets gave up their blockade. Stalin lost this battle of the Cold War, and the West gained new friends in Germany and Berlin.

Berlin Tempelhof Airport remained a vital gateway in the heart of Berlin until the end of the Cold War and beyond. In 2008 however, it was decided to close the airport due to poor economic performance and build a new commercial airport—Airport Willy Brandt, 11 miles southeast of the city center. After considering multiple suggestions for the nearly 1,000 acres of prime real estate, Tempelhof was restored to its original purpose—a park for Berliners to enjoy on weekends and holidays. Where aircraft once took off and landed, where foodstuff and essentials were once delivered, Berliners now can jog, walk, bike, and picnic on the vast grass-covered fields around the runways and taxiways. Being a focal point of leisure, only some of the food trucks have returned to the runways but most of the cafes around Tempelhof have endured a dry spell since the airport closed and the military and civilian ground staff moved away.

"Until the closing of the airport, we'd been a blind spot of the city because of security and fences, which have only just recently been removed. We're now a much more popular destination for people to visit," de Keijzer says optimistically. "However, you come here with a purpose, you don't walk by our cafe by chance. Especially not this side of the former airport." He hopes that just like other parts of Berlin, Tempelhof district will thrive in the future because of its vast opportunities. Almost untouched by gentrification, the area around the former airfield is still looking for a new identity. But de Keijzer knows that because of the attraction of the former airport and its history, people are still willing to come.

Only five minutes from the former airfield, and mostly hidden from mainstream tourism, is Cafe Atlantic. Maintaining a unique identity, the cafe has relied less on visitors or airport personnel for business, and more on loyal Berliners and the many inhabitants of Bergmann Kietz (the area between Tempelhof and Kreuzberg). For more than 30 years, the cafe has remained both unchanged and unimpressed by the waves of coffee experienced elsewhere. "Our regulars expect us to stay who we are, with the same menu and the same coffee—and we don't even accept any form of card payments," says Ibrahim Chahine, the cafe's manager.

Seventy-five years after Mayor Reuter's appeal to the world, it became clear that Berliners were not abandoned. But, sadly, the stage of one of the most incredible operations during the Cold War eventually was. Tempelhof—especially during the winter months—feels like a forgotten place. To keep up the spirit, some coffee shop owners have started a new operation Santa Claus to attract tourists. On Christmas Day, they give out free coffee for the ones who venture a visit at Tempelhof Field. But unlike during the Berlin Airlift, there aren't any children running towards the runways, and only a few joggers escape the cold wind to enjoy an espresso.

—

APPENDIX

Berlin:

19grams
157 Rue Marcadet, 75018
Paris, France

Albatross Bakery
Graefestraße 66/67, 10967
Berlin, Germany

Alte Milch
Eisenbahnstraße 42, 10997
Berlin, Germany

Anna Blume
Kollwitzstraße 83, 10435
Berlin, Germany

Annelies
Görlitzer Str. 68, 10997
Berlin, Germany

August63
Online
Berlin, Germany

Bäckerei Kädtler
Danziger Str. 135, 10407
Berlin, Germany

Ben Rahim
Sophienstraße 7A, 10178
Berlin, Germany

Bonanza Coffee Roasters
Adalbertstraße 70, 10999
Berlin, Germany

Bonanza Coffee Roasters
Alte Schönhauser Str. 15, 10119
Berlin, Germany

Bonanza Coffee Roasters
Jägerstraße 58 - 60, 10117
Berlin, Germany

Bonanza Coffee Roasters
Oderberger Str. 35, 10435
Berlin, Germany

Cafe Atlantic
Bergmannstraße 100, 10961
Berlin, Germany

Café Einstein
Kurfürstenstraße 58, 10785
Berlin, Germany

Café Lina
Lindenstraße 9-14, 10969
Berlin, Germany

Café Sybille
Karl-Marx-Allee 72, 10243
Berlin, Germany

Chapter One
Mittenwalder Str. 30, 10961
Berlin, Germany

CODA
Friedelstraße 47, 12047
Berlin, Germany

Coffee Circle—Bergmannkiez
Bergmannstraße 10, 10961
Berlin, Germany

Coffee Circle—Mitte
Rosa-Luxemburg-Straße 19, 10178
Berlin, Germany

Coffee Circle—Wedding
Lindower Straße 18, 13347
Berlin, Germany

Companion Tea & Coffee
Weserstr. 166, 12045
Berlin, Germany

Distrikt Coffee
Bergstraße 68, 10115
Berlin, Germany

Ernst
Gerichtstraße 54, 13347
Berlin, Germany

Father Carpenter
Münzstraße 21, 10178
Berlin, Germany

Fine Bagels
Warschauer Str. 74, 10243
Berlin, Germany

Five Elephant—KaDeWe
Tauentzienstraße 21-24, 10789
Berlin, Germany

Five Elephant—Kollwitz
Kollwitzstraße 98, 10435
Berlin, Germany

Five Elephant—Kreuzberg
Reichenberger Str. 101, 10999
Berlin, Germany

Five Elephant—Mitte
Alte Schönhauser Str. 14, 10119
Berlin, Germany

Fjord Coffee Roasters
Zur Alten Börse 79, 12681
Berlin, Germany

Gorilla Bäckerei
Hermannstraße 211, 12049
Berlin, Germany

Isla Coffee
Hermannstraße 37, 12049
Berlin, Germany

Jules
Geisbergstraße 9, 10777
Berlin, Germany

Julius
Gerichtstraße 31, 13347
Berlin, Germany

Juno Juno
Weserstr. 165, 12045
Berlin, Germany

Kaffee 9
Eisenbahnstraße 43, 10997
Berlin, Germany

Kaffeebar
Graefestraße 8, 10967
Berlin, Germany

Kaffeeform
Choriner Str. 56, 10435
Berlin, Germany

KEIT
Goltzstraße 18, 10781
Berlin, Germany

KEIT
Grünberger Str. 75, 10245
Berlin, Germany

Kin Dee
Lützowstraße 81, 10785
Berlin, Germany

Kino International
Karl-Marx-Allee 33, 10178
Berlin, Germany

Le Balto
Hobrechtstraße 28, 12047
Berlin, Germany

Lubian Papeterie
Rosa-Luxemburg-Straße 28, 10178
Berlin, Germany

APPENDIX

Man versus Machine
Neue Schönhauser Str. 8, 10178
Berlin, Germany

Motel Minibar
Waldstraße 11a Haus 9 EG, 13403
Berlin, Germany

Motif Wein
Weserstr. 189, 12045
Berlin, Germany

Nella Beljan Gallery
Leipziger Str. 60/61, 10117
Berlin, Germany

Orville's
Platz d. Luftbrücke 4, 12101
Berlin, Germany

Oslo Kaffebar
Eichendorffstraße 13, 10115
Berlin, Germany

Refugio Café
Lenaustraße 4, 12047
Berlin, Germany

Remi
Torstraße 48, 10119
Berlin, Germany

Repeater
Pannierstraße 45, 12047
Berlin, Germany

Rixbox Espresso
Richardstraße 2, 12043
Berlin, Germany

Soultrade Recordstore
Sanderstraße 29, 12047
Berlin, Germany

Röststätte
Ackerstraße 173, 10115
Berlin, Germany

Röststätte
Rosenthaler Straße 40-41 Hackesche
Höfe (Hof, 1, 10178 Berlin, Germany

Salon Babette
Karl-Marx-Allee 36, 10178
Berlin, Germany

Silo Coffee
Gabriel-Max-Straße 4, 10245
Berlin, Germany

Sing Blackbird
Sanderstraße 11, 12047
Berlin, Germany

Taktil
Nogatstraße 38, 12051
Berlin, Germany

THE BARN
Schönhauser Allee 8, 10119
Berlin, Germany

THE BARN—Café Kranzler
Kurfürstendamm 22, 10719
Berlin, Germany

Tischendorf
Friedelstraße 25, 12047
Berlin, Germany

Voo Store
Oranienstraße 24, 10999
Berlin, Germany

Vote Coffee Roastery
Naumburger Str. 4, 12057
Berlin, Germany

Zacharias Kaffeebar
Kollwitzstraße 44, 10405
Berlin, Germany

Zeit für Brot
Alte Schönhauser Str. 4, 10119
Berlin, Germany

Outside Berlin:

Coffee Table Mags
Online—Hamburg

Devoción
69 Grand St, Brooklyn,
NY 11249, United States

La Cabra
Graven 20, 8000
Aarhus, Denmark

Monmouth Coffee Company
2 Park St, London SE1 9AD,
United Kingdom

Sightglass Coffee
301 Divisadero St, San Francisco,
CA 94117, United States

**
*This list represents coffee shops visited,
referenced, or interviewed on background
for the making of Drift, Volume 13: Berlin.*

BERLIN

INSTAGRAM
@driftmag

TWITTER
@driftny

FACEBOOK
/driftny

WEBSITE
www.driftmag.com